PHILOSOPHY OF PSYCHOLOGY

Critical Assessments of Contemporary Psychology
A *Series of Columbia University Press*
Daniel N. Robinson, Series Editor

Philosophy of Psychology

Daniel N. Robinson

COLUMBIA UNIVERSITY PRESS
New York
1985

Columbia University Press
New York   Guildford, Surrey
Copyright © 1985 Columbia University Press
All rights reserved

Printed in the United States of America

Library of Congress Cataloging in Publication Data

Robinson, Daniel N., 1937–
   Philosophy of psychology.

   (Critical assessments of contemporary psychology)
   Bibliography: p.
   Includes index.
   1. Psychology—Philosophy. I. Title. II. Series.
BF38.R59 1985   150′.1   84-23878
ISBN 0-231-05922-1 (alk. paper)
ISBN 0-231-05923-X (pbk.)

Clothbound editions of Columbia University Press Books are Smyth-
sewn and printed on permanent and durable acid-free paper.

To my wife Francine, who asked for this book for many years, and to my daughters Tracey and Kimberley, with love.

Contents

Preface

Not long after I had decided to write this book I had occasion to meet with a former student, now a highly credentialed philosopher with his fingers on the pulse of his discipline. He had, to my gratification, found use for other books of mine in several of his Philosophy seminars and so I thought he would be interested to learn of my plans for this book. "Philosophy of Psychology?" said he; "It's a dead subject!"

I should say that this verdict—this autopsy report—did not come as a complete surprise to me, though it might well discourage readers from proceeding much further. Where intellectual pursuits are involved, "dead" must be regarded as a relative term now stripped of its customary finality. During the long and triumphant season of Behaviorism, for example, the study of Mind was a "dead" subject, but has since returned, through the cognitive sciences, to a position of dominance. To say a subject is dead, therefore, is not so much to describe it as to summarize the interests and attitudes of those who might be expected to nurture it. What my young friend was indicating was the general sentiment within academic Philosophy to the effect that Philosophy of Psychology was not as important as any number of other problem-areas amenable to philosophical investigation. Apparently, most of the influential members of the philosophical community had reached the conclusion that the traditional issues of philosophical Psychology were either wrangles over the meaning of words, or had been dissolved by scientific study or were best understood within narrower and highly specialized compartments; e.g., epistemology, computer science, linguistics, artificial intelligence, sociology of knowledge, etc. On this construal, the *body* of philosophical Psychology had died, but its *members* were still vital.

If philosophers are inclined to see this subject as cadaverous, psychologists tend to regard it as extraterrestrial! After all, what's the point of laboring to develop Psychology as an independent science if, a century later, critics are still proposing philosophical approaches to the subject? Only when psychologists were willing to abandon that armchair of dreamy speculation was there any possibility of a scientific Psychology. The final years of the twentieth century surely cannot be the time to beat a retreat. To many psychologists, then, the "philosophical psychologist" is a strange, anachronistic creature; some otherworldly mutant for whom (or for which) the dividing-line between idle chatter and productive labor is invisible; one who fails to realize that "philosophy" is what psychologists do when their work is done, as others might jog, play chess or refinish old furniture.

But all of this is at an utterly superficial level and can be safely dismissed as little more than an expression of academic fashions. The plain fact is that much of what is now taken to be the leading edge Philosophy is just philosophical Psychology, as is a substantial amount of theoretical and conceptual activity within Psychology. Every month the leading philosophical journals host searching essays on intentionality, free will, thought, justice, aesthetics, moral judgments, belief—the full panoply of issues arising from the facts of human nature, human *psychology*. And for their part, psychologists from dawn to dusk must make at least implicit and *philosophical* decisions on the nature of explanation, causal determinations, the aptness of models and metaphors, the validity of certain constructs, etc. It may be that philosophical Psychology has, as it were, gone underground, but certainly not by burial, and this is what the following pages are intended to make clear.

PHILOSOPHY OF PSYCHOLOGY

CHAPTER ONE

The Armchair
and the Laboratory

For the psychologist working in the penultimate decade of the twentieth century, the subject of *philosophical* psychology is likely to be regarded as purely historical, even atavistic. It was the very subject that had to be abandoned in order that *real* Psychology—"scientific" Psychology—could come into being. Modern Psychology began, after all, only when the armchair and its many comforts were sacrificed for the laboratory and its many burdens. An especially vivid example of this view was provided a few years ago by a well-known experimental psychologist who had just returned from a visit to a mutual friend. "How is X getting on?" I asked.

"Well," said he, "he's going through a mid-life crisis; he's doing a lot of philosophical stuff."

William James, however, knew better. He knew that as Psychology's scientific prosperity grew, so too would its need for philosophical maturity. A *natural science* of Psychology does not mean a nonphilosophical Psychology:

> It means just the reverse; it means a psychology particularly frag-
> ile, and into which the waters of metaphysical criticism leak at every

joint. . . . A string of raw facts; a little gossip and wrangle about opinions; a little classification and generalization on the mere descriptive level; a strong prejudice that we *have* states of mind, and that our brain conditions them: but not a single law in the sense in which physics shows us laws, not a single proposition from which any consequence can causally be deduced.[1]

James, of course, enjoyed eminence both as a philosopher and as a psychologist. He was no enemy of the laboratory; indeed, a good case can be made for his priority over Wundt in this regard. But he also had learned to respect the "armchair" and to appreciate the irreducibly philosophical dimensions of science itself.

Like the aging laborer who returns from his first University class and announces to his wife, "We've been speaking English prose all our lives!" many a psychologist has been immersed in philosophical speculation, if only half-consciously. The very selection of a laboratory as a place in which questions might be answered is a philosophical decision, and a momentous and vexing one at that. It launches the investigator into ever deeper "metaphysical waters," where the aimless voyage is far more common than the charted one. Or, to borrow from the other metaphor, we may say that although psychologists have been speaking prose all their lives, they have not always spoken it well or correctly. No matter how "scientific" the psychological investigation is, there are ubiquitous philosophical aspects of it which, when unnoticed, are likely to be fatally defective.

But the term "philosophical" has very wide extension, often covering nearly anything taking place in the armchair. For present purposes this extension must be restricted so as to exclude both idle speculation at one extreme and purely logical abstractions at the other. Thus restricted, *philosophical* Psychology is confined chiefly to an examination of *meanings*: An examination of what it means to say that an event is caused or explained or somehow understood; an examination of the criteria associated with calling an event a "psychological" one; an examination of the considerations that go into making a question an "empirical" one or fit for experimental modes of address.

At a superficial level we might think that questions of

meaning are settled simply by consulting the dictionary or by establishing how given terms and phrases are used by the native speakers of the language. Such a procedure, however, can yield no more than a "folk Psychology" perhaps useful to the anthropologist. Alas, modern psychological discourse is utterly infected with "folk" meanings and has no dictionary of its own with which to perform translations and corrections. But here we get ahead of ourselves. The point now is that an examination of the meaning of psychological utterances and claims must go deeper than a merely lexical inquiry. Thus, when the psychologist accounts for Smith's behavior by saying that Smith was impelled by "unconcious motives," we are interested in more than the meaning of the words. We are interested at least in what sort of "impulse" is involved and whether it is unopposably determinative. We are interested further in the sort of evidence adduced to support the claim that there are in fact "unconscious" motives and how these differ from those of which the actor is aware. Accordingly, we would be poorly served by the psychologist who offered no more than synonyms when pressed for a clarification.

The choice of a psychoanalytic example might seem self-serving in light of the ostensibly "philosophical" nature of psychoanalytic theory itself. But a similar line of questioning is engaged by the claim that a food-deprived animal is "motivated" or somehow impelled toward behavior of a certain kind. In both instances psychologists are not merely reporting a statistically reliable association between two "variables," but affirming a lawful dependency. Even those who would insist on confining their statements to the observable association itself have adopted a metaphysical position that triggers still other queries.[2] And these too cannot be set aside by dictionary definitions of the terms employed. The psychologist who insists that all utterances be confined to statements of "observables" is accountable and must give reasons for the injunction. As we press on we will discover that a veritable *philosophy of science* stands behind it and that this philosophy itself is not vindicated by "observables"!

To say, then, that the province of philosophical Psychology is the province of *meanings* is not to consign the subject to "semantics" or to argue implicitly that Psychology's problems are no more than verbal quibbles. It is to say instead that any discipline claiming *truth* as an objective is finally a body of *propositions*; propositions regarding method, fact, confirmation, measurement and explanation. These propositions and their logical connectives (i.e., their "if . . . then," "therefore" clauses) yield what may be called the *arguments* of the discipline. The task of philosophical Psychology is to unravel and to test the meaning of these arguments. This is a task that can be deferred but not avoided indefinitely by any discipline that would be taken seriously.

If the task is to be realistic and rewarding, philosophical Psychology must not promise too much. It must not encroach on that exclusively factual territory to which the empirical sciences have laid valid claim. A philosophical inquiry into the meaning of psychological arguments leads to assessments of the coherence of these arguments and not to an appraisal or discovery of the facts themselves. To take a trivial example, we know that when Smith claims to have an "idea of red" he is not claiming to have a "red idea." In recognizing the logical distinction between an idea of X and an X-idea we do not establish *either* factually. Some of the scorn heaped upon the "armchair Psychology" of the past was invited by those who overreached themselves in their otherwise informing introspective activities. But the fact-gatherers have also overreached themselves when, for example, they have moved from what James called "a little classification and generalization on the mere descriptive level" to triumphant conclusions regarding nothing less than the nature of human nature.[3]

Here, too, philosophical Psychology has the essential function of the referee who must determine which moves are permissible. There are, after all, different types of generalization. There is the merely statistical process of extrapolating from an empirically established trend to more distant and untested regions of the same continuum. This is an example of the philosophically neutral induction that yields harmless and often useful predictions. We might call these *horizontal* generalizations and contrast them with the very different *vertical* generalizations that extend to relationships having no or very little empirical support. The horizontal generalizations common to the established sciences (and to the established specialties within experimental Psychology, such as psychophysics) are defended and defensible on the grounds that the fundamental processes governing the relationship are known. For example, the subjective brightness of brief (less than 100 milliseconds) flashes of light is determined by the total energy in the flash. Thus, all other factors being equal, brightness is a function of the product of intensity X exposure duration (I X t), which is the well known *Bloch's Law* of intensity-time reciprocity. Now, *since* it is the total energy (I X t) that determines the effect, we validly generalize (predict) that the same relationship must obtain when flashes of different wavelength are employed; put another way, that Bloch's Law applies to lights of different "color." The inference here is based upon the prior discovery that *energy* is the determinative variable and on the physical fact that energy is a function of wavelength.

　　Vertical generalizations are different, radically more complex, and ultimately depend upon the validity of theories of a higher order. Again for illustrative purposes we may take the fact that Macaque monkeys are known to possess cells in their cerebral cortexes that respond selectively to the shape of their hands.[4] And, at a different level of observation, we discover that human infants display a recognition of their own mothers' faces. But these two disconnected facts would not permit the conclusion that the infant is somehow equipped with cortical cells "pre-tuned" to the physiognomy of that infant's mother. Of course, no one has suggested otherwise. But note what would have to stand at the foundation of such a suggestion were it seriously proposed. Minimally there would have to be strong arguments supporting the expectation that the evolution of the cerebral cortex is nearly the same in monkey and in human being. But this very expectation would rest on still other methods for determining— without *assuming* the validity of the theory—the degree to which two different developmental processes are "nearly the same." It is not necessary to become involved with this particular issue to appreciate how different this sort of generalization is from the one based upon Bloch's Law in vision. In the latter instance the same effect (perceived brightness) is the subject of the generalization and the same physical continuum (energy) is taken to be the determinative independent variable for the same observer. But with vertical generalizations such as the illustrative one we confront two different *species*, two different and not merely "physical" classes of stimuli ("distress" calls and human vocalizations), and two different patterns of behavior (cell discharges and the infant's orienting responses). Thus, to expect that the same processes are involved is first to accept the validity and generalizability of that very evolutionary theory the findings would tend to support or challenge.

What philosophical Psychology has to contribute here is partly a reminder and to some extent at least a *conceptual* corrective. Only rarely, however, are such contributions of the neat and unarguably logical sort. That is, it is only rarely (one must hope) that psychological discourse is formally self-contradictory or fallacious. And given the fact that psychologists, too, are rational beings, it would not be necessary to depend upon the separate discipline of Philosophy to discover blatantly fallacious arguments or self-contradictory propositions. Philosophers do not have and do not claim proprietorship of logical coherence. What they do have are the benefits of a self-imposed discipline in the matter of cutting away the purely "folk" features of argument and getting at its fundamental conceptual assumptions and claims. Like the angel Ithuriel in *Paradise Lost*, Philosophy has an instrument designed to disclose the true nature of whatever it touches. But the analogy here is much too brazen. It is more apt to say that philosophical modes of analysis help us preserve whatever truths (better, *facts*) have been independently gathered as we insert these facts into more general propositions and arguments to which these facts are judged to be germane.

It should be clear by now that philosophical Psychology is not offered as a panacea or a magicians's wand. Rather, it is a harbinger of conceptual dead-ends; an after-the-fact pathologist who helps to explain what killed a theory; a schoolmaster who, often tediously, insists on the proper grammatical forms; a patient translator who assists interlocutors in the important business of making themselves intelligible to one another; and *occasionally* an expert witness summoned to instruct the court as to whether a regulative maxim of logic has been violated.

In these various roles philosophical Psychology has always been at least an implicit part of psychological and scientific research and theory, just as Psychology itself has been an implicit part of nearly all of Philosophy except for Logic. The traditional topics of Philosophy—ethics, metaphysics, political philosophy, social philosophy—proceed from any number of *psychological* assumptions; assumptions about human motivations and goals; about human perception and belief; about human penchants for aggregating. Typically these assumptions are drawn from a combination of the philosopher's own (introspected) "nature" and from a general if imprecise notion of how other human beings have tended to behave in various circumstances. Thus, both the philosopher and the psychologist have, as it were, "been speaking English prose" all their lives; both have been *philosophical psychologists*, but in different ways. It may be true, as A. J. Ayer once said, that "Philosophical theories are neutral with respect to particular matters of fact"[5] but this is so only because of the formal propositional manner in which the theories are assembled. When the philosopher attempts to put together an argument for the "just state," the originating principle of the argument may be to the effect that human beings are by nature "self-interested." To turn up a few persons who may be said not to be thus "self-interested" is never sufficient to overturn the theory, since the theory itself claims validity only to the extent that the (theoretical) occupants of the state are in fact self-interested. Thus, if A. J. Ayer meant only that the *form* of philosophical theories and the (logical) methods of testing their coherence are neutral as regards matters of fact, we can surely concur. But at some point the theory takes on the burden of both prediction and explanation, and what it would predict or explain is some *matters of fact*. Perhaps at this point we would be inclined to take it now not as a philosophical but a scientific theory. Be that as it may, its author is no longer neutral!

Even if it is established, however, that philosophical Psychology is an implicit part or in the background of contemporary efforts in Philosophy and Psychology, the question still lingers as to whether this hybrid is itself a discipline or merely one of the tools used somewhat differently within two distinct disciplines. Are we to think of philosophical Psychology the way we think, for example, of physiological or sensory or developmental Psychology; or should it be regarded as Statistics is—as a separate if indispensible "device" for settling questions of a certain kind? This is the sort of question that is surrounded by necessary equivocations. Statistics, let us recall, is also a branch of mathematics and is developed in abstract and formal ways by specialists who need never consider experimental findings. Logic, too, is both a formal and an abstract discipline unto itself *and* a practical device for drawing boundaries around rational discourse. One man's tool is another man's science.

As with Statistics and Logic, the specialty of philosophical Psychology is likely to be a tool for the many, a science for the few. In this book it is treated only as a tool; as a set of guidelines for clarifying certain concepts, for assessing certain strategies, for weighing the merits of certain arguments. In many instances, this "tool" is seen to be nothing more than clear thinking. Indeed, one is inclined to describe, if not define, philosophical Psychology as *the habit of clear thinking* about psychological issues. But a statement of this kind is arrogant and offensive if not qualified. *"Read this book if you would think clearly"* is scarcely the way to appeal to an intelligent audience of students and teachers! When I refer to *habitual* clarity of thought I am suggesting the refinement of a talent that already exists, and not one that remains to be acquired. There is a symmetry, then, between the habitual clarity of thought imparted by philosophical Psychology and the habitual clarity of method imparted by experimental Psychology. What the student is expected to derive from the latter is a *refinement* of just that talent for precision, care, and problem-solving that is already present, but that has not yet become habitual. The analogy holds all along the way. The trained experimenter knows that repeated measurement is necessary if the effects of the indepen-

dent variable are not to be confused with merely statistical fluc-
tuations in the phenomenon of interest. The aim here is not to
be misled by coincidences, not to be confused by "noise." The
philosophical psychologist knows that to have the idea of "blue"
is not to have a "blue idea." But in both instances, the specialists
are not in possession of dark truths that are inaccessible to ordinary human intelligence. Uneducated gamblers since remote
antiquity have known enough to be suspicious when the dice keep
yielding "7" and "11" or when the favored stallion falls asleep in
the starting box. Belief in miracles is an ageless fixture of the human experience, and the concept of a "miracle" is available only
to those with the prior concept of probabilities. So, too, with "blue
ideas" and the like. Who has ever required tuition in Philosophy
lest he think that, in recalling an elephant, there is an elephant
in his head? To accept that there is, in fact, an external world is
at least implicitly to accept a distinction between the act and the
object of perception and thus between the attributes of the act
and the attributes of the object.

But although the gamblers of history have known that
a long run of "7"s and "11"s is odd—that something is amiss—
it was only with the advent of probability theory and Statistics
that we could quantify the oddness. And it only through that habitual clarity of method we call *experimentation* that we can quantify
the confidence we are allowed to have in the effects one variable
has on another. When we turn to philosophical Psychology the
expected benefits are similar, though not expressible numerically.
The benefits are expressible chiefly by example. What are taken
to be the more important examples are given in the balance of
this book.

In choosing such examples it is important to focus on
the genuinely philosophical features of psychological thought; on
what are sometimes referred to as the "meta-psychological" aspects rather than the psychological aspects *per se*. The latter are
appropriately assessed within the context of critical appraisals of
specific psychological "systems" or theories or programs of research.[6] But to choose one set of features over and against others
is philosophical work in its own right and proceeds from a class-

ification, the principal terms of which warrant discussion. Just how do we recognize an issue or premise as philosophical rather than, say, psychological or scientific?

Again, I would draw attention to the distinction between the factual claims and utterances—the *arguments*—of a discipline and an analysis of the *meanings* properly attached to these. The meanings arise from what is finally the metaphysical foundation on which such claims are based. As used here, "metaphysical" refers to two distinguishable though reciprocally informing classes of questions or premises; viz., the *ontological* and the *epistemological*. Ontological questions refer to the existential standing of an entity or process. Thus, whether or not there are bona fide mental events is an ontological question. Epistemological questions arise when we adopt a critical attitude toward the very modes of knowing that are brought to bear on any question. Obviously the stand we take on the ontological status of an entity or process will be determined by our epistemological presuppositions and *vice versa*. To ask, for example, if mental events are *real* (as opposed to being just physical events by another name) is simultaneously to ask for a certain kind of evidence; but this itself presupposes the validity of a given mode of inquiry.

There is a vicious circularity in all of this that is to some extent unavoidable. The ontologist who insists that only *physical* entities have real existence is confronted by an adversary who declares that, in addition to physical entities, there are mental ones whose attributes include the one of being nonphysical. The stage is now set for the gathering and weighing of relevant evidence. But suppose at this juncture the physicalist insists that only public evidence—only occurrences able to excite the sensory and perceptual processes of neutral observers—will be accepted. Clearly, this condition begs the very question at issue, since only physical occurrences can have sensory effects. We shall have much more to say on this specific matter in a later chapter. I use it here to illustrate the subtle and the not so subtle ways that ontological and epistemological claims are intermingled. When we take a position on what there is, unavoidably we also take a position on how we ever know what there is. Together these ontological and epistemological considerations establish the metaphysical boundaries within which the central arguments of a discipline are developed. They are the considerations that permit at least a thin line to be drawn between the philosophical and the nonphilosophical contents of psychological discourse.

The line, however, is a thin one and resists attempts to make it permanent. We learn, for example, that "Beatrice appeared to Dante in his sleep," and we begin to plumb the meaning of this claim. What sort of entity appeared to Dante? The obvious answer is that "Beatrice" here refers not to an actual person but to some sort of apparition, a kind of hallucination common to dreamers. The only proof we would require is that Beatrice was somewhere else at the time Dante saw "her." But in this case we would only be taking one first-person account ("I saw Beatrice at dinner with her parents.") over Dante's account ("I saw Beatrice in my sleep.") Let us say, however, that dozens of people saw Beatrice at dinner with her parents at just the time Dante was sleeping and "seeing" Beatrice. We, and presumably Dante too, would now be satisfied that the Beatrice of the dream was not *really* Beatrice but just a figment of Dante's dream-world. The position we have taken is one of common sense at one level but is also metaphysical at another. We have agreed to confer ontological standing only on the Beatrice publicly observed and to withhold it from the entity seen only by the dreamer. But how is this strategy to work when, for example, a Copernicus insists that the sun is stationary at a time when every man, woman, and child sees it rising and setting every day? In the case of Dante's dream we were willing to settle the matter by appealing to the methods of social science. We conducted a poll, as it were, and discovered that reliable witnesses all saw (the *real*) Beatrice somewhere else at the time Dante claimed to have seen her in his room. But the Copernican claim also refers to a publicly verifiable phenomenon: To wit, that the sun does not move.

The example should not be misconstrued. It is, of course, trivially true that Copernicanism was subsequently confirmed by achievements in astonomy and astrophysics and that the Ptolemaic alternative, which was in closer accord with common experience, was shown to be false. But the example is getting at something quite different. In the matter of Dante's dream there was never any doubt that the public record would settle the question. And, in the matter of Copernicus' thesis, there was never any doubt that the ordinary facts of perception would *not* settle the question. Note that Copernicus, too, "saw" the sun rise and set. Note also that the heavens would look the same to an earthly observer whether the observer adopted the Copernican *or* the Ptolemaic perspective. We might grant that some of the resistance to Copernicus was based on scripture and some of it on the layman's conviction that a moving earth would be felt to move. But in every knowledge-claim there is this element of conviction or belief as well as the element of one or another sort of experience. These are the *psychological* concomitants of epistemic claims but they must also be taken into *philosophical* consideration. Again, sharp and permanent lines between the two may be chimerical. If we insist that the intensity of belief is a psychological factor that has no bearing whatever on the *truth* of what is believed, then we are prepared to accept that belief is neither a necessary nor a sufficient condition of truth. More generally, we are prepared to accept that *nothing* of a purely psychological nature has any bearing on the truth-value of various philosophical claims. But perception itself is "purely psychological" and constitutes the very essence of so-called empirical modes of verification.

It has become customary to avoid the pitfalls of an utterly subjective epistemology—to resist "psychologism"—by qualifying the role of belief in assessments of knowledge-claims. Thus, Smith is said to know X when Smith believes X and has *good reasons* for so believing.[7] This scarcely strips the enterprise of psychological attributes, however, since to have a good reason is, among other considerations, to believe one has a good reason or at least to have a reason many others believe is a good one. The qualification accordingly simply substitutes a sociological for a psychological standard. We might adopt a conciliatory and pragmatic attitude here and just not worry about the classification. But the consequence is likely to be (as it has been) a very false sense of security within Psychology and Philosophy. In the last analysis it *does matter* whether the armchair or the laboratory is the proper setting for inquiries of a certain kind. To the extent that a question, properly understood, is a metaphysical one whose answer turns on conceptual as opposed to factual considerations, psychological and scientific approaches will be nugatory and misleading. If only for tactical reasons, therefore, it is advisable to defer the "research program" long enough for the necessary metaphysical groundwork to be performed.

    This is not to say that Psychology is to sit still for some indefinite period during which Philosophy will legislate the psychologist's agenda. As already noted, philosophers and psychologists have been doing each other's work wittingly or otherwise all along. There is no formula, no incantation, no magical potion for discovering who is to have custody of "truths" about this or that. An undergraduate, after a few courses in Psychology and proper instruction in statistics and experimental design, can undertake original research and bring it to a sound and an informative conclusion. As with any endeavor, experience is a good teacher; but one need not have a doctoral degree to undertake acceptable research. Nor must one be a professor of Philosophy in order to think clearly about a set of questions. Philosophical Psychology is not, then, a compound-subject to be apportioned to two distinct groups, but one subject to be cultivated by all interested parties in an ongoing and organic way and not in sequence. Whether or not it is to be cultivated well depends chiefly on the resourcefulness of those engaged in the work. In this there is no substitute for each worker's willingness to learn how the other's tools are used. The philosopher who insists, for example, that an orange afterimage is just like the experience produced by a real orange-colored object placed before the eyes[8] would have had second thoughts had he known that the subjective size of an afterimage varies with the distance between the experient and the background onto which the afterimage is projected (Emmert's Law). But our perception of an external object does not behave in any such manner. The point is not that the entire philosophical argument collapses once this psychological fact is known, but that the argument itself might have been richer or might even have taken a different turn in light of the fact that after-images and veridical perceptions behave differently. And the computer scientist who regard the central question in artificial intelligence to be the nature of "the symbols in the brain"[9] certainly would have benefited from the reminder that there are no symbols in the brain at all; only in the things we say about the brain! Again, this corrective is not at the expense of the entire specialty of artificial intelligence. Rather, it is an aid to those who would develop coherent arguments in favor of this specialty and its implications for an understanding of human intelligence.

The message here becomes clearer when we examine again the differences between Dante's dream and Copernicus's claim. If we regard both at a merely superficial level of meaning there appears to be no difference at all. Dante is found to be insisting that he saw Beatrice while Copernicus declares that the earth is moving. But as it happens the two utterances are entirely unlike. What Dante is reporting is no more than *a fact of experience*, whereas Copernicus is presenting *the conclusion of an argument*. The question raised by Dante's report is whether or not his experience was tied to an external property of the world (e.g., the property of having Beatrice occupying a specific location at a specified time). In other words, what we want to establish when Dante says that he say Beatrice in his room is whether this fact of experience is also a fact about the world or is *merely* a fact of experience. Accordingly, we take it as decisive that other and equally reliable persons saw her elsewhere when Dante had the experience of her presence in his room. As stated, Dante's utterance is no more than—and was intended to be no more than—a bald empirical announcement pertaining to private sensations. While accepting that Dante had such sensations, we reserve the right to determine whether their cause was external to Dante or arose entirely from purely internal and even eccentric features of Dante's unconscious or physiology or brain-states.

But the Copernican claim to the effect that the earth is in motion is of a very different sort and, as noted, is not an empirical claim at all, since Copernicus's "experiences" are in this regard no different from anyone else's. Copernicus does not declare that he *feels* the earth moving or that he *sees* the sun to be stationary. If pressed on the point, he will insist not merely that the earth moves but that the earth *necessarily* moves, its movement being the necessary deduction of an argument whose major premise is nothing less than a law of science. Dante saw Beatrice because of something unique to Dante. And so Dante's claim is finally a description of Dante. Copernicus's claim is not a description at all and thus is not to be settled by appeals to perception alone.

At a certain level we are inclined to treat Dante's dream as a psychological phenomenon and Copernicus's thesis as "scientific," but there is a question-begging dimension to this. Suppose, for example, that Dante—after learning that others had seen Beatrice somewhere else—insisted that there might be two Beatrices (perhaps identical twins) or, more boldly, that *his* Beatrice was as *real* as any other, and not just to him. Let us impute this argument to Dante:

1. All knowledge-claims are grounded ultimately in the facts of experience and are, therefore, "private" at least to the extent that any experience is some specific person's experience.

2. Such experiences are made possible, in the last analysis, by particular states and processes within the brain of the experient.

3. The states and processes within Dante's brain at the time he saw Beatrice in his room were identical to those states and processes occurring when an (allegedly) "external" Beatrice is perceived—by Dante or by anyone else.

4. The mere fact that the states and processes corresponding to "Beatrice" happened to occur in the brains of a number of people in a restaurant has no bearing on the validity of *Dante's* brain states. All that can be said is that the brain-equivalents of "Beatrice" occur in many different brains and they happened to occur in Dante's (at home) while they were also occurring to others (at a restaurant some distance from Dante's residence).

The question now is whether there is still a clear distinction to be made between "psychological" and "scientific" accounts. But note that now Dante's position is radically different from a simple claim to the effect that he saw something. For as a result of 1–4 above, Dante is adopting a *theoretical* position regarding his experiences. He is no longer content to report what he has seen, but has been forced to develop a theory to account for it. At this juncture his authority disappears and his utterances must come to satisfy criteria that are independent of his particular psychological attributes. As long as he confined himself to truthful reports of *his own* perceptions he enjoyed the special authority that comes from each of us having sole proprietorship of our own experiences. But, once he found it necessary to develop *arguments* to account for the experiences, he entered a different epistemic realm; the realm in which propositions, facts, implications and logical entailments merge to form testable hypotheses. He moved from the private duchy of his own personal "psychology," through the "waters of metaphysics," and on toward a scientific (in this case, neurological) theory that would explain all phenomena in terms of brain-states and processes.

There is a lesson to be drawn from the saga of this fictionalized Dante, apart from the obvious one that teaches us not to confuse a fact of private experience with a scientific proposition arising from the laws of science. The more subtle lesson is that the realm of private experience is as well defended against scientific encroachments as science is against encroachments from the other side! As we shall have occasion to discuss later in the book, this is a lesson not well learned by modern Psychology. Too often it is proposed or suggested that a scientific account of the *mechanisms* by which experiences occur is at once an explanation of the experiences themselves. The implication is that a theory which accounts for the occurrence of an event is, at the same time, an exhaustive account of the nature of the event; that an explanation of *how* something comes about is identical to an explanation of *what* that something is.

The confusion is less common where inanimate objects are involved. In invoking the gravitational laws to explain *why* a pencil falls, we don't pretend to explain *what* a pencil is or what its uses are. But psychologists are not as careful to notice the difference between an analysis of the causal sequence leading up to the experience "blue" and an explanation of the experience *as an experience*. As we shall see, this conflation of *how* with *what* has driven psychologists and philosophers to any number of peculiar onto-logical positions, not the least surprising of which is the denial of mental events.

   Let us recall also Quine's second "dogma of empiricism"[10] which would reserve meaning only to those utter-ances that can be completely reduced to specific (sensory?) ex-periences. We can share Quine's impatience with the woolliness of reductionistic theses of this sort without adopting his prefer-ence for behavioristic alternatives. As I have discussed at some length elsewhere,[11] there is all the difference between a *percept* and a *concept*, the latter being an entirely propositional affair which may be and very often is "contentless"; e.g., the concept of *the largest positive integer*, or the concept of *the square root of minus* 1. Recurring once more to Dante's dream, we can say that, in referring to Be-atrice, Dante was reporting a *percept* whereas Copernicus, in refer-ring to a moving earth, was offering a short-hand account of his *concept* (his *conception*) of celestial dynamics. The "reductionism" criticized by Quine would attach meaning to this account only to the extent that it could be completely translated into specific em-pirical (experiential) elements. But, as the terrestrial experiences are exactly the same whether one adopts a Ptolemaic or a Co-pernican perspective, reductionism would be found claiming that the Ptolemaic and the Copernican accounts *mean* the same thing!

   Contemporary psychological discourse has moved some distance away from radical empiricism, but even in its most ex-otic "cognitive" form this discourse still remains tied to one or another variety of reductionistic thinking. We shall have much more to say on this in chapter 3. It is sufficient here to call attention to the essentially philosophical nature of the attachment and therefore to the need for essentially philosophical modes of analysis in any attempt to assess it. A concept such as "the larg-est positive integer" is likely to be treated even by cognitive psy-chologists as the result of generalized learning or induction; i.e., as the terminus of a continuum formed through (empirical) con-tact with one's, two's, three's . . . *n*'s. It is, of course, entirely possible that some persons have no more than this in mind when they refer to the largest positive integer but, if so, they do not in fact have the concept of the largest positive integer, for "the largest positive integer" is not a number, nor is it the terminal point on the continuum of positive integers. There is no "largest positive integer," only the *concept* of such. The ontologist may be content to treat such concepts as mere "truths about words," as Hume suggested, but their *psychological* importance remains unaffected by their ultimate ontological fate. If there "really" is no square root of minus 1, except in our conceptual life, the psychologist must still account for it. It cannot be regarded as a species of hallucination (like Dante's Beatrice, for example) simply on the grounds that there is no experience that corresponds to it. Nor is it "subjective" in the sense of arising from eccentricities of the cognizer.

Let me close this phase of the discussion by noting only that our rapidly developing "cognitive Psychology" has yet to recognize the special status of concepts and has therefore failed to develop methods of examining, let alone explaining, them. On the side of explanation, the cognitive specialties have tended to pass off what are seldom more than metaphors or similes or allegories that attempt to describe or suggest what thought is "like." Such accounts contain the ubiquitous "process," but it is not at all clear what a "process" is, except that it is somehow "like" the "processes" occurring within a computer or a brain or a telephone switchboard. We have now learned to accept that some of these "processes" are "unconscious" and that they even pass through discrete "stages" of "cognitive development." This is all quite hopeless, of course, and it would seem to be one of the missions of a mature philosophical Psychology to begin to unravel such knotted locutions.

In saying that it is time to *begin* this work I do not mean to imply that we are at ground-zero, but that we have been in something of a coasting pattern for the past two or three decades. Most of the philosophical energies within Psychology were spent on critiques of Behaviorism and, as of this date, there seems to be only a partial recovery from the war of words. The "new" cognitive sciences are to some extent retracings of an older "mentalism" that the behaviorists had attempted to bury. Even some of our "pioneering" research could have been done—and, on a less than generous construal, *was* done—in Wundt's laboratory![12] If we are to move ahead in research and theory, we must move ahead in our conceptualizations of the discipline. If there was something defective in the older mentalism, we are scarcely going to repair the defect merely by doing the same research with better equipment or by analogizing the findings in the idiom of computer technology. And even if we decide to continue our business as usual, it is important that we know that we are doing so and why we are doing so.

CHAPTER TWO

Determinism, "Hard" and "Soft"

" **H**appy is the man who knows the causes of things," says the ancient maxim, though we may wonder if its author appreciated the great confusion and ambiguity surrounding the concept of *causation*. Nonetheless, the concept traditionally has been at the very center of our notions about science and scientific explanations. Even in this, our metaphysically tutored age, we generally regard a body of knowledge as scientific when it contains *causal* accounts of why things are as they are or come to be as they come to be. We would modify the old bromide to read, "*Scientific* is the enterprise that establishes the causes of things." But now we must ask, *What sort of entity is a cause*? When we say, for example, that apples fall toward the center of the earth *because* of the laws of gravity, what meaning is to be attached to this "because"? More generally, how are we to understand assertions to the effect that a given event was *determined* to occur when and in the way it did?

As will be made clear, deterministic philosophies have had a troubled history in general and continue to be plagued by mixtures of incoherence, tautology, and contradiction. Psychology has not only borrowed from but has also contributed to this history whose liabilities are at the foundation of many of our current confusions. The following illustrate how psychologists make use of causal language:

1. Smith forgets where his keys are because of a temporal-lobe tumor.
2. Smith forgets where his keys are because of repressed hostility toward the person he must drive to visit.
3. Smith is forgetful because of a reinforcement history that failed to reward attentiveness.
4. Smith's memory lapses result from a neurotic disturbance.
5. Smith is easily distracted, nervous about travel, and therefore often misplaces things when he is about to undertake a journey.
6. Smith forgot his keys because he has a lot on his mind.
7. Smith lacks the motivation it takes to keep track of things.
8. Smith's memory-deficits are part of a general intellectual deficit arising from a mild retardation.
9. Smith's father was forgetful, too!

These nine attempts to account for the phenomenon provide examples of the most frequently employed causal or deterministic approaches taken by modern Psychology. The approaches are grounded in neurological hypotheses (1), or psychoanalytic theories (2), or theories of conditioning (3), or notions of psychopathology (4), or personality "types" (5), or models of "information-processing" (6), or theories of motivation (7) or of intellect (8), or theories of psychological heritability (9). But in these and related forms, the attempts seldom derive benefits from anything resembling a critical position in the matter of the implied or explicit causal relations. Instead, psychologists tend—with more than a trace of unintended irony—to adopt "scientific" conventions regarding causation, even though the latter are of that peculiar Humean stripe that is *psychological* from start to finish. It will be instructive to review Hume's famous and influential theory of causal determinations.

Aristotle and Hume on Causation

To appreciate the dimensions of Hume's achievement, we should remind ourselves of the Aristotelian model that Hume's all but completely replaced, at least within the modern sciences. I say *Aristotelian* by way of acknowledging any number of notions grafted on to Aristotle's original formulations. Together, the original formulations and their various additions and refinements may be taken as the Rationalist tradition in the matter of causality.

Aristotle argued in several places[1] that earlier philosophers had an incomplete conception of causation and were thus at a loss to offer or even discover the principles covering a complete explanation of any natural event. Such an explanation, he insisted, would have to begin with an appreciation for the differences among knowing *that*, knowing *how*, and knowing *why* something is the way it is. He sought to repair the older and defective view through his fourfold theory of causation, the famous theory of *Material*, *Formal*, *Efficient*, and *Final* causes. According to his model, we have not given a full causal account of, for example, a house merely by specifying its (material) composition or by pointing to the structural (formal) principles it satisfies. Nor, however, is the account completed once we have listed the entire series of physical actions performed by the builders. Their effects on the materials constitute the efficient cause in the way that the effects of hammer and chisel on stone are the efficient cause of a statue. But if the complete causal explanation of a house is to be given, it is further required that we include the architect's plans, objectives, goals—in a word, the *end* (*telos*) toward which all the various actions were performed. This ultimate purpose is realized last in time (it is "final" in this sense) but conceptually first.

Aristotle himself, unlike a number of later Aristotelians, was careful to note that the Final Cause may be the Good or may only be the *apparent* Good toward which the chain of events proceeds.[2] He employed the concept in a variety of contexts, somewhat differently in each. We may surmise, for example, that he had the Atomists and their radical materialism in mind when he insisted that, *if the art of shipbuilding were in the wood, there would be ships by nature.*[3] His point, of course, is that, no matter how long pieces of wood are exposed to the purely natural elements, the fully fitted trireme will never be thus produced. If there is to be a trireme, there must be an intelligent and intending agent to organize purely physical actions in such a manner as to have such a ship *made.* In his ethical writings, the Final Cause surfaces as the ingredient of *intentionality* allowing the moral character of actions to be assessed by permitting distinctions among intended, unintended, and accidental outcomes.[4] In his political treatises the same concept is deployed when we are called upon to judge the various forms and modes of political organization. It permits us to recognize what is essential to the proper assessment of governments; *viz.* the *ends* to which statecraft is committed, whether the form of government is oligarchic, monarchic, democratic, etc.[5]

A vital question arising from such a theory pertains to the kind of relationship that exists between events and their (fourfold) causes. The pivotal consideration here is supplied by the concept of *necessity.* Aristotle is extremely cautious on this issue. He does not want to be charged with arguing that, for example, it rains *so that* the corn will rot on the threshing floor![6] He approaches the question, therefore, with an analysis of the concept of necessity in Book II of his *Physics.*[7] There are at least three senses of the word "necessity": the *logical,* the *definitional,* and the *hypothetical.* The first is illustrated by the connection between a conclusion and the premises of a valid syllogistic argument. If the premises are true and if the form of the syllogism is valid, *necessarily* the conclusion is true. Definitional necessity is found in mathematics where, for example, the sum of the angles of a triangle equals a straight line. Or, to take a different example, in instances of synomymy such as, "All unmarried men are bachelors *necessarily.*" Now, the relationship between the "that for the sake of which" (the end or goal or *telos*) and the specific steps taken to achieve it is neither logically nor lexically necessary. There are, after all, many different ways of building a house such that "house"—as an end—does not *logically* necessitate any given step.

Nor is "bricklaying" or "masonry" synonymous with "house." Rather, the relationship between, on the one hand, the material, formal and efficient causes and, on the other, the Final Cause is one of *hypothetical necessity*. If there is to be a house, *necessarily* this and that must be done, this and that must exist, etc. As Aristotle says, in asking why a saw is the way it is,

> It is, therefore, necessary for it to be of iron *if* we are to have a saw and perform the operation of sawing. What is necessary then, is necessary *on a hypothesis*; it is not a result necessarily determined by antecedents. Necessity is in the matter, while "that for the sake of which" is in the definition. (*Physics*, II:9)[8]

In saying that the "that for the sake of which" is in the definition, Aristotle calls attention to the fact that a word like "house" carries with it such functions as shelter, safety, location. Every house serves certain common ends, and thus the word "house" necessarily implies functions of a given type. Here we have the feature of definitional necessity. Now, in building a house, if we are to build it of a certain size and in just so much time, *necessarily* we must have tools for cutting wood. The house is not necessarily determined by such antecedents as woodcutting. That is, it is not necessarily determined the way the conclusion of a syllogism is necessarily determined by its premises. Aristotle notes in the same chapter that there is often a mixture of definitional and hypothetical necessities. Thus the word "saw" refers by definition to properties of just the sort that are necessary *if* certain objectives are to be met; e.g., dividing hard substances such as wood.

No end of misunderstanding has been spawned by a passage in the same essay which finds Aristotle saying, "It is plain then that nature is a cause, a cause that operates for a purpose."[9] Regarded in a certain light it seems to anticipate a Spinozistic necessitarianism which, in fact, Aristotle would have rejected out of hand. For Aristotle not everything that happens *in nature* is natural, nor are the ends of natural events unfailing. As there are accidents in art, so too are there accidents in nature. When we discover monstrosities such as the "man-faced ox progeny" cited by

Empedocles, we don't inquire into the "that for the sake of which" such creatures occur. They are *errors*; as we would say today, defects in the genetic template. For Aristotle, then, what is *natural* is that outcome which is nearly invariable; that which, with very few exceptions, is the culmination of ontogenetic processes under nurturing conditions. It is simply wrong to attribute to Aristotle the theory that *everything* that happens is for some "end" or, worse, that *everything* that happens is for the "Good." From his claim that there is purpose in nature it is impermissible to conclude that he believed nature had purposes. "Nature" here is akin to "art," not to the *artist*. Whether there is, as it were, an artist behind the arts of nature is a separate matter.

The seeds of controversy were sewn, therefore, not by Aristotle's "rationalism" (such as it was) or even by his teleology, though there is room for energetic discourse on both of these. The idea that would become central to Hume's critique was, instead, the one expressed in such passages as, "Necessity is in the matter. . . ." It was this notion of a material necessity that suggested the real existence of causal forces, powers, properties inherent in things. At this point it may be more useful to retreat from Aristotle's own words and the theory arising from them and turn to what may be called the *Aristotelian* tradition in the matter of causal "powers" and their (controversially) *necessary* effects.

If the task at hand, referring to our example, is cutting wood, we will of course take recourse to a tool that is harder than wood and sharp. Experience teaches that finely honed steel teeth will make short work of timber. And experience here is exceptionless. Such instruments *always* cut through wood. In other words, the relationship between the properties of the saw and the disintegration of the lumber is not accidental. What sort of relationship is it, therefore? More generally, just what is the relationship between cause and effect if not a *necessary* one? It surely isn't accidental, for if it were the outcome would be statistically indeterminate.

Let us take the traditional trichotomy applied to observed events. We say that "X" occurred either by chance or not by chance and, if not by chance, then by . . . ? By what? The third possibility is either *necessity* or *contingency*. The second of these alternatives is ordinarily invoked when "X" is neither a logical inevitability nor a necessary definitional truth. Thus, we say the occurrence of "X" is a *contingent* occurrence when, in fact, no canon of logic would be violated had "X" not occurred. It is (merely) contingently true that animals with kidneys are animals with hearts; it is surely not necessary. And it is (merely) contingently the case that of all the ways green plants could manufacture their cells, the process of photosynthesis is the one actually involved. It is imaginable that a green plant could nourish itself without photosynthesis, but it is unimaginable that a false conclusion results from true premises in a valid syllogistic argument; just as it is unimaginable—it is *impossible*—that some bachelors are married.

But is it just the case that the sharply honed steel teeth of a saw cut through wood and that a rubber hose does not? That is, is it merely contingent that the effect of sharpened steel on wood is what it is? Metaphysics in the patrimony of Aristotle answered this in the negative. Since the causal sequences in nature are nearly invariant—and, in fact, are invariant except where there is a defect of some sort in the causal agency—it is clear that causes *necessarily* have their effects. When Aristotle declares, therefore, that "Necessity is in the matter," he is acknowledging that certain material attributes necessarily have the effects they have. He is not quite as innocent about this as later disciples would be, for he notes, as pointed out above, that there is often an inextricable connection between definitional and hypothetical necessities. It is fair to say that, to some extent, Aristotle would have accepted the proposition that even his "material necessity" is viciously tautologous. The proposition could be defended thus: (a) An exhaustive definition of "saw" must include the attributes of hardness and sharpness; (b) an exhaustive definition of "hardness" and "sharpness" must include relativistic qualifiers such that something has the attributes of hardness and sharpness relative to entities having less of each; (c) through a thorough classification of real objects according to their relative densities and shapes, all items answering to the name "saw" are given higher standing in hardness and sharpness than items answering to the name "wood."

These confidences would begin to shake in the last decade of the seventeenth century and crumble by the middle of the eighteenth. The process began innocently enough with Locke's attempt at a "Newtonian" Psychology; an essentially *corpuscular* theory of mind in which associative principles operated in a manner akin to gravity. The details of this Psychology are not relevant here but several of Locke's arguments in its behalf are. We can set aside the improbable claim that Locke was committed to refuting Descartes's (alleged) theory of "innate ideas"[11] and we can also break the habit of treating Locke as a radical "empiricist." Locke proposed a number of "original acts" of the mind (each of them coming as close to "innate ideas" as anything proposed by Descartes), and left ample room for *intuition* and *demonstration* in his catalogue of the human modes of knowing. Where Locke's famous *Essay*[12] caused a crack in the foundations of the official Metaphysics was in his distinction between primary and secondary "qualities" of things. His arguments against perceptual *realism* were influential, if defective. He developed a very strong case for the claim that perceptual modes of knowing involve not merely *reactions* to the physical properties of external objects, but *transactions* by which the consequences of perception are not reducible to or images of their physical antecedents. Our idea of hardness, for example, is fashioned out of sensations of the "primary" quality of an object; viz., its density. That is, the sensation matches the objective attribute. But our idea of "blueness" arises from a transaction between a property (not a "blue" property) of the object and a property of the mechanisms of color vision. "Blue," therefore, is a *secondary* or *derived* quality, not a *primary* or *directly given* one. The perceptions in both cases are caused by the physical attributes of the external "objective" body or event, but the knowledge that is tied to secondary qualities is not direct knowledge of the physical attributes that produce them. Put in our modern idiom, we would say that persons with normal vision see "blue" but they do not *see* wavelengths.

It remained for George Berkeley to perform his surprising intermediary step to set the stage for David Hume. Berkeley's metaphysics is a complicated affair which must be neglected here.[13] It is enough at this point to see how he out-Locked John Locke, and how he did so with reasonings as tight as their results were (and are) implausible. If, as both Locke and Descartes insisted, we do not have *direct* knowledge of an external world but only direct knowledge of our own sensations (call them perceptions, ideas, conscious events), then *all* knowledge is of (Locke's) "secondary qualities." It makes no sense at all to claim that we experience hardness because an object is, in fact, hard but that we experience "blueness" for some other reason. In both cases what we experience can only be the contents of our own minds. Years later and more rigorously, Kant would make the distinction between things as in themselves they *really* are (their *noumenal* reality) and things as they are known by us *phenomenally*. Kant would reject Berkeley's so-called "subjective idealism" but would, in the process, neglect Berkeley's subtle distinctions. We will not tarry to explore the full range of implications Berkeley drew from his critique of Locke. One of the implications is, however, worth noting. Referring to Newton's extraordinary discovery of the Universal Law of Gravitation, this utterly consistent philosopher tellingly insisted that he could find nothing in the Law "signified besides the effect itself."[14] Enter Hume.

Hume's treatment of causation is developed both in the *Enquiry*[15] and his A *Treatise of Human Nature*,[16] works that have had unparalleled influence on Philosophy in the English-speaking world. His argument in both texts is empiricistic and phenomenalistic, the net effect being to convert the concept of causation from a metaphysical to a psychological one. The conclusion of his arguments may be briefly stated thus: The reference of causal attributions and of "necessary connections" is the experiential history of the observer and not the external physical events themselves. Thus, to say that A is the cause of B and that B results necessarily from A is, on Hume's account, not a description of what an observer actually *sees*, but an inference—an implicit theory—forged out of a number of similar perceptions in the past. We come to regard A as the cause of B after frequent exposure to events of the A-type being followed by events of the B-type. Whenever the criterion of *constant conjunction* is faithfully satisfied, we impute causation to the pairings. And in regarding as *necessary* the dependence of effects on their "causes"—the dependence of consequents on their antecedents—we are acknowledging only that the conjunction of the two has been exceptionless in our experience.

In relocating the reference of causal statements Hume "psychologized" both science and metaphysics. In the Rationalist tradition, statements to the effect that "A is the cause of B" referred to something—some power or agency—in "A" and "B." But in the Humean tradition, the same statements actually refer to mental associations forged out of current and prior experiences. The same is the case with "necessity." To say that causes *necessarily* have their effects is either to utter a definitional truth (which cannot add in any way to our knowledge of the real world) or to make the purely historical claim that these particular antecedents have *always* been followed by these particular consequents in experience; in *everyone's* experiences. Causality and necessity, therefore, are not "out there" but are productions or expressions of certain habitual tendencies of mind. He defines "cause" in the *Treatise* as,

> an object precedent and contiguous to another, and so united with it, that the idea of the one determines the mind to form the idea of the other, and the impression of the one to form a more lively idea of the other. (p. 170)

The "so united" refers, of course, to *constant conjunctions* which provide the conditions by which our mental associations are formed. When such conditions prevail we ascribe causation to the event-sequences. Hume's otherwise odd claim that, therefore, "anything may produce anything"[17] follows logically from his theory of causation. Our minds, after all, could have been so constituted that we could only sample events once each minute rather than more or less continuously. The creature that gets a glimpse of the world only once per minute, and only for, say, 100 milliseconds of each such sample, would surely have a radically different scheme of causal dependencies. In a word, *whatever* A is, it will be taken to be the cause of B, *whatever* B is, when A and B have been constantly conjoined in experience.

Through long seasons of refinements, and notwith-standing its many and well-known defects to the contrary, Hume's theory of causation came to be adopted by the natural sciences. John Stuart Mill's influence here was very great, for he recast the Humean model in a form that yielded the *experimental* methods suitable to the discovery of "causes."[18] The triumph of Hume's position is to be understood largely as the result of the zeal with which nineteenth-century scientists shunned all that was "meta-physical." A totally empiricistic model of causation—a model in which only observable "objects" figured in the causal language of science—was an effective way to keep mere philosophy out of the precincts of experimental science. Psychology, of course—always eager to adopt the perspectives and methods of the developed sciences—was "Humeanized" in that century and has remained so in very nearly all of its experimental forms and in most of its theoretical and explicative efforts. It is not surprising, therefore, that when psychological explanations are *deterministic* they are causal explanations of the Humean sort. An examination of these must begin, then, with an appraisal of this nearly official Humean model.

Causal Explanations

Thomas Reid was but the earliest to recognize some of the defects in Hume's account[19] and he has been followed by a veritable legion of critics ever since.[20] It is doubtful that many philosophers today would regard themselves as unflinching dis-ciples of Hume on the matter of causation, though a large num-ber would declare and have declared that Hume was at least on the right track. For the sake of brevity, it is sufficient here to ig-nore the differences between Hume's own statements and those that have arisen from them or that have been offered as improve-ments. Instead, all of them can be treated as instances of a *regu-larity* theory of causation according to which the concept of "cause" refers ultimately to the perceived statistical reliability obtaining between (prior) A-type events and (later) B-type events. A causal *law*, then, is just the shift in tense from statements of the form, "A has always been followed by B" to the form, "A-types are followed by B-types." Statements of the form, "A is the cause of B" are then regarded as pithier versions of all of these. Nothing "necessary" is involved in any of this, however, necessity being reserved for exclusively logical rather than natural relations.

Reid rejected the regularity thesis on the grounds that it is disconfirmed by the only two kinds of evidence that could support it. There are many instances of sequential regularity that are never taken to be causal *and* there are singular sequences that are immediately recognized as causal. No one regards day as the "cause" of night even though the two are constantly conjoined; nor is anyone doubtful as to the cause of his own actions even when these are performed for the first time. We need not do something over and over again in order to ascertain that we are (probably!) the cause of its happening. Nor does the notion of generalizations or inferences from past experience help here, for we could only generalize from the first instance if we already took that instance to be one in which we were the cause of our own actions. Reid was inclined to think that it was just our own sense of ourselves as agents having the *power* to bring things about that gave rise to the notion of "causes" or agencies in nature. But in any case, he found no evidence to support Hume's insistence that perceived regularities exhaustively explained causation.

Quite apart from the psychological evidence telling for or against the regularity thesis there are conceptual difficulties as well. To equate causes and effects with "objects"—and here Hume could only be referring to objects of perception—is finally to be vulnerable to the (Kantian) argument according to which perception itself is regulated by the nonempirical ("pure") contexts ("intuitions") of time and space, and is accordingly not willynilly. To speak of an "event-sequence" is to speak of temporally ordered and spatially organized happenings that are explicable only in terms of "causal laws," as it were, that are never the result of experience. If A is perceived as occurring earlier in time than B this must be because either (a) it does occur earlier or (b) the nuances of information-processing by the brain or mind result in its being

perceived as occurring earlier or (c) both (a) and (b). But the per-
ceiver has no evidence at all of (b), nor any independent means
by which to gather such evidence. All an inquiry into this subject
can yield is the imposition of the very same nuances on the inquiry itself. That is, the inquiry could never produce discoveries
of the sort, "Aha! I believed that A preceded B because of the way
my mind processes information, whereas I now know (see?) that
A actually follows B!" On Hume's account, therefore, we are required to regard the perceived sequence as the actual sequence
because we have no empirical grounds for claiming anything about
how the mind works *internally*, since these workings are never perceived; they are never "objects." But this leaves us only with possibility (a); viz., that A is perceived as preceding B because, in fact,
it precedes it. But to precede it, A must occupy a position in time
different from the position occupied by B and this difference in
residency is *necessary* for A and B to occur distinguishably. Thus,
for there to be two "events" there must (i.e., necessarily) be distinguishable spatial and temporal residences for each. And for one
of them to be "earlier," it must be "earlier" in a way that is independent of our perhaps eccentric but forever undiscoverable
modes of *knowing* it is earlier. For ordinary mortals, therefore, *for
whom the laws of perception or of cognition cannot be shown to be wrong by
any method involving perception and cognition*, the regular movement of
A-type events to B-type events is perceived to take place because
it *does* take place, and any negation of the proposition could not
be *empirically* intelligible even if conceivable. That is, an empirical
instantiation of the counterargument is impossible. But if the
empirical instantiation of the negation is impossible, then the initial
proposition is necessary. This is surely what Kant's famous *Second
Analogy* is getting at:

      "Everything that happens, that is, begins to be, pre-
supposes something upon which it follows by a rule."[21]

      It may be argued that the "necessity" here arises from
(the admittedly incontrovertible) peculiarities of human knowl-
edge-modes and that some other kind of creature would, in a
manner of speaking, see things differently. Be that as it may, we

could never discover this *empirically*, meaning that its demonstration could never be presented as either an "object" or an "event."

It is important to make the distinction between causal laws being necessarily what they are (which is false) and causes necessarily having the effects they do. Ohm's law is not necessarily true, for it is possible for current, voltage, and resistance to be related in ways different from the way expressed by the law. But *if* Ohm's Law is true then the effect of changing the resistance in a circuit is a necessary effect. This is so for entirely unsurprising syllogistic reasons. But that the change in resistance must *precede* and the change in current *follow* is also necessary, and not for (merely) syllogistic reasons. When we say that the current in a circuit is, *ceteris paribus*, determined by the resistance we are not uttering a tautology but explaining just those causal relations that define a circuit. A circuit is nothing more than and no different from a collection of objects whose electrical behavior is determined by Ohm's Law. The inclination among philosophers, at least since the time of Hume, is to regard such determination as "contingent," meaning thereby that although it is not accidental it is also not necessary. "Contingent" here means the determination could have been otherwise, whereas with necessary determination it could not have been otherwise. The inclination, that is, is to regard all necessity as logical, never natural. Accordingly, "X is necessary" only when the proposition *not*-X is a formal contradiction.

Some, however, such as William Kneale[22] and George Molnar[23] have revived an interest in the necessitarian theory of natural laws chiefly through damaging assessments of the common alternative. Borrowing from Popper the example of a fictitious creature, the "moa," who dies before reaching its fiftieth year, Molnar offers the case of there being only one such creature in the history of the world, and this one accidentally dying at an age less than fifty. We now have just the empirical grounds on which to declare as a law of nature, ALL MOAS DIE BEFORE REACHING FIFTY! In attributing the death of the only moa to an accident, we might only be admitting ignorance of just what killed it. But even if we isolated the condition leading to its death, we surely could not say that such conditions kill moas for there has only been one such moa. But the larger point is well made in Molnar's concluding passages:

> If it is conceivable that a particular sequence is accidental, then it is conceivable that a regular sequence should be accidental, even if the regularity is on a cosmic scale. This is the basis of our feeling that the description of laws as contingent empirical generalizations, true independently of local conditions, fails to reveal what it is about laws that enables them to limit possibilities. Such generalizations state that something is universally just so, and I cannot see, as Kneale could not see, how something's being just so can make its not being so impossible. The case of the inexplicable *and* accidental death of the lone moa therefore ought to be admitted as a counterexample to the analysis of law under discussion.[24]

The causal laws of nature *do* limit possibilities; e.g., the relativity laws render it impossible for anything to move faster than light. But empirical generalizations set no such limit on the possible. The difference between relativity laws and empirical generalizations is not to be found in the observational realm. We do not say that nothing travels faster than light simply because we've never seen something traveling faster than light but because we take the limit to be expressive of a law of nature. But from the empirical fact of that lone moa's death at age 49, we do not take as a law of nature the proposition, "All moa's die before 50."

In the present context it is not important to make out a case for or against necessitarian theories of causation. It is enough to indicate that a purely descriptive and correlational approach to the explanation of natural phenomena leads to counterintuitive results. There is, we must suppose, something *determinative* about causal laws, even as we remain metaphysically neutral as to "powers," "hidden forces," and "agencies." We are inclined to take the determining "agency"—call it what you will— to be the source of those Humean constant conjunctions, while recognizing that not all such invariances are instantiations of causal determination. "Correlation," as the introductory psychology texts affirm, "does not imply causation."

On the necessitarian view, but no less on the Humean view, causal factors are a matter of public record and require nothing of a purely personal property of observers. It is trivially true, of course, that Humean causation is a perceptual affair, but not in the solipsistic sense of being exclusively "my" or "his" affair. And on the more formal construal of causal laws, the causal sequences are taken to be "true in all possible worlds," as the expression goes, if all possible worlds are physical in the sense that ours is; that is, in all worlds in which specifiable initial conditions obtain. Needless to say, actual observers need not inhabit these other worlds for the causal laws to operate. Exit Berkeley.

At this point we can turn our attention to various deterministic models within Psychology, recognizing that the success of any of them requires the satisfaction of certain minimal criteria. First, the model must be grounded in or must make appeals to causal laws of just that sort that *limit possibilities*. The sense in which the regularity theory allows "anything to be the cause of anything" is precisely the sense in which strict Humean causation *cannot* be at the roots of deterministic models. No correlation, no matter how great, implies causality, nor does any correlation, no matter how great, legislate against exceptions arising from still other samples. The law-type statements of a deterministic model are *nomic*, not descriptive. They are proscriptive and not permissive. And, unlike empirical generalizations, laws of causal determinism are able to absorb and in no way be embarrassed by contrary-to-fact conditional statements. No number of astronomical observations and generalizations based on them would permit one to say that, if the Earth's gravitational forces were eliminated, the moon's trajectory would cease to be elliptical. It is just in the nature of empirical generalizations that they are generalizations from what has obtained. There is no room for what would have been the case had what we observed been radically different from what it was. Again, causal laws in science, in limiting possibilities—including unobserved and *unobservable* possibilities—are as applicable to counterfactuals as to actuals. Thus, psychological determinism, expressed in the form of determinative causal laws, must also accommodate counterfactuals, meaning among other considerations that it must be based upon something different from descriptive statistics!

Finally, determinative causal laws in Psychology must be aloof to "private" evidence and private epistemic states. This requirement will become clearer when "authenticity" is discussed within the context of free will. But to leave this part of the issue announced but unaddressed, it is enough to say that the psychological determinism proposed must be no more beholden to what the observer has to say *about himself* than would be physical determinism in the inanimate realm.

Determinism

There are so many and such varied arguments for determinism that it is hazardous to discuss the concept without first indicating the sense in which the term is used. Richard Taylor, in the *Encyclopedia of Philosophy*, offers a general definition that provides a good starting point:

$[D_1]$ "DETERMINISM is the general philosphical thesis which states that for everything that ever happens there are conditions such that, given them, nothing else could happen."[25]

The key notions in this general definition are "conditions" and "could," for these are the notions that tend to permit distinctions among the several formulations of determinism.

Consider the legend told of the baseball umpire Bill Klem. As the tale goes, he had just called "strike three" when the irate batter hurled his bat in the air. Klem declared, "If that bat comes down, you're out of the game!" That, in fact, the batter's ejection was inevitable is guaranteed by the laws of gravity. Thus, referring back to Taylor's definition, we can say that the relevant "conditions" in this case are just those gravitational laws coupled with the promise that, should these laws hold, ejection will follow. But note that the batter's ejection is actually determined by more than one sort of "conditions." Assuming the validity of the gravitation laws, the bat's descent is deductively certain. But it is not certain that Mr. Klem might not "change his mind" during the interval. Then again, suppose baseball's rules contained the provision, "A batter who intentionally throws his bat more than four feet in any direction shall be ejected from the game." Now we have added a "condition" (a *rule*) that renders the batter's ejection *inevitable* by rendering Mr. Klem unable to "change his mind."

What this vignette provides are two instances of inevitability, but instances that are entirely unlike. There is, first, the inevitability of the bat's descent, determined by causal *laws* in Physics; and there is the inevitability of the batter's ejection determined by the proscriptive *rules* of the game. The obvious point here is that events or occurrences can be inevitable in more than one way and that, therefore, inevitability cannot be sufficient to make the case for the determinism now under consideration. The determinism we must address is the one that covers both natural laws and conventional rules; the one that regards not only the bat's descent as inevitable but also the invention of the game of baseball and the rules that will govern it, as well as such events as an umpire's "changing his mind." It is the determinism that covers, in Taylor's words, *everything that ever happens*.

Historically, the most common objection to this variety of determinism has come from those who regard the human will to be free and therefore to be exempted from coverage. But before examining arguments of this sort, it is important to consider more recent (twentieth-century) objections arising from the alleged indeterminacy of purely physical events. The objections are based on the well-known Heisenberg Principle according to which *uncertainty relations* have ontological status and are not merely the result of experimental or technical limitations. It is just in the nature of subatomic particles such as "wavicles" that the actual relationship between position and energy is indeterminate and not merely undeterminable. Indeed, the relationship is necessarily undeterminable because it is indeterminate.

If we suppose that this principle of modern quantum mechanics is true in some ultimate sense, then surely the deterministic thesis as defined by Taylor is false in that there is no set of conditions able at once to guarantee both the location and the mass-energy of at least some states or "things" or events. Such a truth would limit the range of phenomena covered by determinism but it would leave entirely untouched the question of psychological determinism or deterministic laws of Psychology. The immunity of the latter to the truth of such uncertainty relations arises from two considerations. The first is that defenders of psychological indeterminism or of freedom of the human will never have equated either "indeterminacy" or "freedom" with statistical phenomena or as kindred with such notions as "chance," "randomness," "anarchy," and the like. The freedom asserted is, instead, the result of human *agency* and is inextricably tied to human motives, purposes, rationality, and ends. As the particle physicist would not judge uncertainty relations as arising from *choice*, advocates of human freedom regard choice as the very linchpin of their arguments. Secondly, the causally determinative laws of science remain applicable to macroscopic phenomena despite the hypothesized indeterminacy of subatomic relations. For example, the sense in which Ohm's Law is determinative is unaffected by the "indeterminate" nature of events *within* those electrons whose overall behavior establishes the voltage, current, and resistance properties of the circuit. Whatever else may be said of those events regarded as relevant to the question of human freedom, all of them have in common at least the property of being *macroscopic!* In light of these two considerations, it is not useful to challenge deterministic theories of human psychology with notions or even with "truths" known to be applicable only at the level of particle-interactions. Instead, we should take the deterministic thesis as asserting,

$[D_2]$ For everything that ever happens at the level of observable human behavior, there are conditions such that, given them, nothing else could happen.

Great care is required, however, lest this modified thesis be construed in such a way that it is no more than a tautology. Again, the key terms are "conditions" and "could." Let us take the case of Smith's going to the opera. If the claim asserted in (D_2) is that *anyone* whose entire history, from the moment of conception to the moment that Smith leaves for the opera, is exactly the same as Smith's must also leave for the opera, then the claim is tautologously true, for such an "anyone" would be indistinguishable from Smith. Indeed, for "anyone" and "Smith" to have *identical* histories—including time-space identities, genetic identities, etc., "anyone" and "Smith" would be the same entity. The care required, then, is what protects us against accepting a logical truth as an empirical proof. We must regard "conditions," therefore, as *scientific laws* that apply indifferently over all happenings of the type under consideration. The laws governing Smith's going to the opera are the same as those governing Smith's going *anywhere* or anyone going anywhere, in just the way that Ohm's Law covers all simple circuits. If there are such laws, then Smith could not but go to the opera. His behavior in this instance is regulated in quite the same way as would be his falling at an acceleration of 32 feet/sec./sec. were he dropped from a height. Understood this way, (D_2) is the statement of HARD DETERMINISM.

Ever since Donald Davidson's *Actions, Reasons and Causes*[26] there has been a richer awareness of how the traditional arguments against psychological determinism might be dealt with, though Davidson's own position has not been entirely static.[27] Before exploring these recent proposals, we should clarify further the conceptual and empirical points of entry that modern (and not so modern) Psychology has created for the deterministic thesis, D_2. The most welcoming conceptual point of entry is the simple fact that significant human actions are not random, but bear a coherent relationship to specified goals. If only in the venerable Aristotelian sense, then, Smith's actions are, as it were, determined by Smith's objectives through a *hypothetical* necessity. But since the objectives themselves have been caused—in just the way Smith's hungers, thirsts, and more general needs are all caused—it follows that Smith's actions have been caused by those externally established conditions within Smith to which his behavior is a response.

That many actions are thus caused has never been seriously disputed, but the requirement of D_2 is more demanding than this. It requires the rejection of such claims as, "Smith *chooses* at least some of his objectives, and his choices here are not determined in the required sense, for they are "determined" by Smith's moral autonomy." In a word, there are some objectives allegedly arising from Smith's *free will*. Let us refer to this as the *voluntarism* thesis and denominate it V. The burden of determinism thus becomes one of establishing either that V is false or that it is, in fact, compatible with D_2. A special set of arguments has been spawned by the second of these possibilities. Collectively these arguments produce the thesis of Compatibilism, C, which may be generally expressed thus:

$$[C]$$ There are causally necessary and sufficient conditions for all human actions that are "free" in the sense required by V.

The defense of C, as shall be discussed, takes the form of showing that V and D_2 can be jointly asserted without contradiction. Thus, at least some voluntarists can be compatibilists. But some cannot. The latter are those subscribing to a (hard) voluntarism of this sort:

$$[V_H]$$ Actions are free if and only if the actor's choice intentionally expresses reasons and beliefs that are authentically his.

What V_H asserts is "hard voluntarism" which rejects both D_2 and C. It rejects D_2 for transparent reasons; it rejects C through the requirement of *authenticity*. As the term is now employed by philosophers,[28] it makes a distinction between those reasons or beliefs of a person's that have been externally supplied or imposed or are otherwise "determined," and those which are not thus derived. The distinction is between some attribute or psychological disposition being merely "his" in contrast to being "his own." When an infant is christened "George," for example, the name becomes "his," but not in the authentic sense of his having freely chosen it. Thus, it is "his" but not "his own." The burden that must be borne by V_H is, among other considerations, arguing successfully for the *authenticity* of an actor's freedom or the authenticity of those personal states or elements that dispose the actor to this as opposed to that course of action. The distillation of what has been said so far is this: D_2 *denies the authenticity of human action sequences and* V_H *affirms it.* Accordingly, C is not contradicted by V but is by V_H.

We are now in a position to give some shape and content to the notion of *soft determinism* which, at least since the time of William James, has been largely dismissed or ridiculed. On the face of it, what "soft" determinists seem to aver is that V_H and D_2 are (somehow) compatible. John Stuart Mill in the last century[29] and B. F. Skinner in our own[30] offer two examples of "determinists" in the odd position of exhorting us to accept (choose) their proposals! Neither's arguments have succeeded, but it is not clear that every argument for a "soft" determinism must be incoherent. I shall return to this later in the chapter, where concepts such as freedom and autonomy are considered not as abiding attributes of this or that *species* (or even this or that human actor), but are states arising within systems that are not entirely "closed."

Reasons and Causes

The distinction between reasons and causes is a venerable one and has been defended in one or another form by Aristotle, Leibniz, and Hegel, to mention just three luminaries.[31] It is a distinction that can be made in a variety of ways but these can be collapsed into a more or less official version of the following form:

Causes are purely natural phenomena in which the element of "agency" is neither discernible nor necessary. *Reasons*, on the other hand, entail "agency" and create a category of *agent-causality* quite unlike the *event-causality* of the physical world. Significant human actions are unintelligible in the absence of an account of the *reasons* behind these actions; the motives, desires, expectations, and objectives framed by the actor and impelling just those actions capable of realizing the actor's purposes. Thus, for example, a *causal* account of the death of Smith might be confined to the (natural) fact that Smith's aorta was punctured by a bullet, but the full explanation of Smith's death would have to include the motives (the reasons) that led the assailant to commit the lethal action. Similarly, all genuinely social and historical events are inexplicable except through the concept of reasons (motives), for we can never account for historical and social episodes by confining attention to merely physical properties of the persons and places involved. To the extent that events can be exhaustively accounted for by taking recourse only to physical descriptions, the events are simply not "historical" or "social" at all; they are "natural."

We can develop a more precise distinction among compatibilists, determinists, and voluntarists using this general statement of the "resons vs. causes" argument. The defenders of D_2 will reject the categorical separation of reasons and causes and will insist that "reasons" themselves are *caused*, and that the causes of "reasons" are drawn from utterly natural-physical sources. Accordingly, there are not "reasons," as such, but certain effects produced in actors and referred to as "reasons" for want of a scientific understanding of their origin and nature. The compatibilist defending C is prepared to accept that there are reasons in the accepted sense of the term, but that natural-causal conditions bring them about. On this construal, a person may be said to act on the basis of reasons, but the reasons themselves are not something over which the actor has total control, nor are they something of his own making. Like other mental entities, reasons too are supplied from the outside—are *learned*—and are not "authentic." Thus, in the sense in which authenticity has already been used, we can say that an actor's reasons are *his* but not *his own*. Finally, the defenders of V_H accept the *reasons-causes* distinction fully and grant to the actor the authentic authorship of at least some actions which, therefore, are explained through *agent-causality*.

The most obvious rejoinder to advocates of V_H is that

an actor's reasons, ultimately understood, are in fact conditions within the actor—conditions of a neural or biological nature—such that the actual causes of the action are physical, although the actor himself is unaware of this. The general problem of *psychophysical reductionism* will be taken up in the next chapter. Without anticipating that analysis, it is enough to note the special problem of reductionism when applied to the reasons-causes issue. The advocate of V_H here is under no obligation to accept any given theory regarding the "ultimate" sources or even "causes" of the actor's reasons. What V_H asserts is that some actions are the consequence of reasons and that the actor, in acting upon these reasons rather than others, takes his actions to be the result of his own choices. Now here a subtle element enters, for we are called upon to ask whether there is any difference—germane to V_H—between an actor being free to act upon his reasons and merely *believing* he is free in this respect.

Let us take the example of a driver who enters a race in which the competing vehicles are (apparently) assigned to drivers randomly. As it happens, our driver—we shall call him A. J. Foil—has been given a car equipped with a computer that actually determines the velocity and acceleration of the vehicle at every point in the course of the race. When Foil presses down on the accelerator, there is a response, but the response is not proportional to Foil's behavior. It is, instead, governed by a computer program. When the race is over, Foil complains that he "tried everything to get the car moving, but something seemed to be holding it back." When we ask Foil whether or not he was under instructions to drive the way he did, or whether his experiences as a driver made him less able to reach top speed, or whether he was under some internal pressure of fear or doubt that prevented him from doing what he knew he should be doing, he tells us no, no, and no. In a word, he claims that everything he did was done *freely*.

The distinction that is relevant here is between (a) freedom defined as the absence of externally imposed constraints on one's *actions* and (b) freedom defined as the absence of externally imposed constraints on the *consequences* of one's actions. Mr. Foil was free in the first sense and not free in the second. This is a basic distinction in that, were Foil not free in the first sense, then we would have good reason to believe that he was unfree *simpliciter*, even if he thought otherwise. But let us assume that instead of tampering with his car we put a drug in his food that would slow down his voluntary and reflexive movements. Moreover, in monitoring his every action during the race, we learn that on each turn—and contrary to the rules of the race—he shouted epithets at the other drivers—doing so, he tells us later, because of his frustration at not being able to drive as well as he customarily does. We can say that the cause of his frustration was the effect of the drug, but that his reaction to his own frustration was something he could have controlled. Thus, we would not hold him responsible for his performance as a driver, but we surely could hold him accountable for his lack of sportsmanship, since the latter is not the invariable consequence of the former.

To this point, two different distinctions have been made: a distinction between constraints on actions and constraints on the consequences of actions; and a distinction between induced internal constraints and their effects on the one hand, and on the other induced internal constraints and effects that are not causally tied to them, even if understandable in terms of them. Whereas we would refer to the drug as the *cause* of Foil's poor performance, and therefore part of the causal chain that led to Foil's frustration, the drug must be regarded as nothing more than a *condition*—neither necessary nor sufficient—under which conduct of a certain kind (e.g., unsportsmanlike behavior) becomes understandable. Note, however, that in jointly establishing two criteria—the criterion of a *condition* that renders behavior understandable, and the criterion of a condition that imposes internal constraints on an actor—we have still not defeated V_H as an account of the unsportsmanlike actions. Accordingly, it is not enough for defenders of either D_2 or C to show that certain physiological conditions are reliably antecedent to certain actions regarded by the actor as "freely" taken. They must show in addition that still other conditions or parts of these conditions were *causally* efficacious in producing both the specific behavior *and* the actor's belief that this specific behavior was freely performed. What is involved here is something like posthypnotic suggestion where the suggestion includes admissions by the actor that the hypnotically performed actions were "free" and where the actor additionally is rendered amnesic with respect to having ever been hypnotized.

There is, then, a difference between freely *doing* and freely *choosing to do.* The usual (reductionistic) rejoinders to V_H are based on proofs that the doing was constrained while leaving the element of choice neglected. However, there have been frontal attacks on *choice* as well by those who have challenged the *authenticity* of the actor's desires, motives, and/or beliefs. This is a more recent literature that repays close examination.[32] It is supportive of a species of C, though its tendencies are clearly in the direction of D_2. I have alluded to it a few times already and I should now state the authenticity-challenge more precisely:

An action is *authentic* in the sense required by V_H if and only if the motives, reasons, or other factors warranting the action are framed by the actor independently of external constraints, compulsions, or coercions, or of internal constraints, compulsions, or coercions over which the actor does not have conscious control.

In treating of authenticity, Robert Young has referred to an agent's "reflective powers" (p. 576) and has argued that, even though a given motive or desire was initially established by conditioning, the agent remains autonomous as long as he is able to "identify" with the conditioned desire in his "reflective judgings" (p. 573).[33]

Note that Young and a number of compatibilists do not deny that an actor's motives are brought about by conditioning or "socialization." Rather, they insist that the resulting actions can still be regarded as autonomous if the actor has so assimilated the motives as to make them *his own;* i.e., if the motives or reasons are *authentic.* Suppose, for example, the actor has habitually displayed aggressive behavior toward his supervisor and, in the course of a successful psychotherapy, comes to recognize that his enmity toward any form of authority was caused by an especially troubled relationship he had had with his own father. Now that he can reflect on the sources of his aggressiveness, he is able to judge it as irrational when directed willynilly at those who happen to have positions of authority. Thus enlightened, he can regulate his responses to internal states that had heretofore triggered angry behavior. Moreover, even when he does give vent to his passions, his behavior is now autonomous because he understands the conditions promoting it. The desires are now really *his own* in that he enjoys full, conscious, and comprehending proprietorship of them.

Compatibilism of this sort has attracted its share of criticism. As Mark Bernstein has written, a proponent of D_2 when faced with an example such as the one I've just provided,

> would hardly be stymied. He would counter by saying that the newly acquired knowledge is just more grist for the socializationist mill. That is, this enlightened person might be so socialized such that when he notices what processes caused him to have certain motivations, he will inevitably and unavoidably accept or reject his motivational make-up.[34]

Yet, there is a feature of the *authenticity* criterion that has not been noticed, though it would seem to enjoy a certain immunity against this sort of criticism. Recall that the challenge to D_2 comes from the proposition that some of an agent's actions are autonomous in that they arise from *authentic* predispositions. What is central to this claim is that the predispositions are the agent's own and not merely installed by conditioning or socialization. They are his own in the sense, for example, that a pain is *his own* whereas his name is merely *his*. But, like his pains, the agent's motives too have a certain "protected" status once the owner claims them. When someone claims to have a toothache, for example, he enjoys a very special epistemic authority that he does not enjoy when making claims about any empirical fact external to himself. To be satisfied that someone has a toothache, we must have at least the evidence of *his* report to that effect. (We would not say, "You have an intense toothache, but you don't know it!") The formal statement of this is that observers' first-person reports of sensations are *incorrigible* in that they cannot be shown to be wrong through methods external to the observers themselves.

What is interesting about the incorrigibility thesis in the present context is that *authenticity*, on any construal, is an attribute that cannot be established independently of the agent's own statements, feelings, beliefs. That is at some point in the evidentiary phase, we need the agent's first-person reports as to the (alleged) authenticity of a feeling or motive or desire or goal. But if his reports are to be regarded as relevant to the question of authenticity, they must be accepted as *autonomously* given. (We must assume, to take a trite example, that there is no one behind the curtain threatening to kill the reporter unless he says this or that.) Thus, the only empirical test of D_2's challenge entails the very autonomy that D_2 denies. But if, in fact, the defender of D_2 insists that no act—including verbal reports of desires or goals—is autonomous, the D_2 thesis turns out to be unconfirmable and irrefutable in principle and is therefore not a scientific thesis at all. It is not even an empirical generalization or "statistical law." To put the matter in the form of an orderly argument, we can say that,

1. Autonomy, A, requires authenticity, A'.
2. A' refers to the relationship between an agent's actions and his predispositions P.
3. P are internal states associated with such items in awareness as reasons, desires, feelings, and beliefs.
4. P may be either *imposed* (by conditioning, socialization, coercion, etc.) or *adopted*, the former symbolized as P_i and the latter as P_a.
5. The ultimate empirical verification of any P (whether P_i or P_a) is in the form of first-person reports, R.
6. For evidence to count as verifying, R must be uncoerced.
7. There is at least one P associated with uncoerced R's if D_2 is testable.
8. Thus, (7) implies P_a; P_a implies A'; A' implies A.

If, for example, (7) is denied, then (5) is impossible and D_2 is untestable in principle. What we see, then, is that any—the word is *any*—empirical test of D_2 entails the validity of V by assuming the existence of A' and therefore A.

Reasons as Causes

It would seem that "reasons" must survive at least as an explanatory device and that some actions must be regarded as taken autonomously in that they proceed from authentic motives or ends on the part of the agent. But this still leaves open the question as to the nature of the relationship between reasons and actions. To say that Smith acted *because* he had a reason is to appeal to some sort of causal account, and so the question has to do with the sense in which this "because" is to be taken.

In his immensely influential essay, *Actions, Reasons and Causes*, Donald Davidson[35] argued for reasons *as* causes and expressed the optimistic view that traditional explanations based upon an actor's reasons would be ultimately transformed into the more common naturalistic (causal) explanations of science. Davidson's later retreats from this position[36] have retained the view that reasons are still somehow like causes or function as causes, even if they cannot be absorbed into the explanatory framework of the natural sciences. When we describe someone as acting on a reason, says Davidson, our explanation includes "the idea of cause, and the idea of rationality. . . . The advantage of this mode of explanation is clear: we can explain behavior without having to know too much about how it was caused. And the cost is appropriate: we cannot turn this mode of explanation into something more like science."[37] But the alleged advantage of retaining reasons is scarcely comforting on Davidson's account, in part because such explanations cannot be turned into scientific ones. But even more damaging than this limitation is the dubious or trivial nature of these "reasons" explanations when they are tied to the notion of the actor as an intending agent. Davidson's important argument on this point may be summarized thus: Let us assume that Smith does X and that, in an attempt to explain X, we say, "Smith must be understood as an agent with reasons and intentions, and the action X was brought about by this (his) agency." The central question here is whether this sentence actually adds anything to the bald empirical utterance, "Smith acted." That is, do we know anything through the longer sentence that goes beyond the information conveyed by the pithier one?

Davidson's analysis first examines whether there is a difference between the action X and "Smith caused X." Those who would insist that the latter is distinct from the former must assume that "Smith caused X" is itself an action of some sort functionally related to X. But then we have the vicious condition of an action being necessary for an action, *ad infinitum*. That is, if "Smith caused X" is itself an action, then we will need a "Smith caused W" as an earlier and necessary action for "Smith caused X," and a "Smith caused V" as the precondition for "Smith caused W," etc. An infinite regress ensues such that any action will not occur until an infinite series of earlier ones has been completed. The only alternative to this, Davidson has argued, is to regard "Smith caused X" as just a somewhat psychologized version of "Smith X'ed," the latter stripped of notions of agency.

The success of this analysis is, however, only apparent and is grounded in assumptions of a dubious and question-begging nature. Only if reasons were causes—only if genuine *actions* were the merely physical effects of earlier physical events—would it follow that an action is necessary for an action, *ad infinitum*. Although casting himself as a compatibilist, Davidson actually must subscribe to a version of D_2 when he insists that an agent must perform an action to perform an action. But it is just this line of argument that defenders of V_H oppose. To say that Smith is an *agent*—to say that at least some of his actions arise from physically undetermined and irreducibly rational considerations—is to say *at least* that his "agency" is not *caused* in the ordinary sense of causation. When we attempt to explain *Hamlet* by referring to Shakespeare's plans, reasons, beliefs, intentions, and aspirations, we mean to say more than, "Shakespeare wrote *Hamlet*," unless, of course, "wrote" is given its wider (and proper) meaning. In the narrow sense of "wrote," there is no way to distinguish between what Shakespeare did four centuries ago and what someone is now doing when he sits down and copies the words of the play. Nor does a criticism of "agency" amount to much when it rests on the problem of infinite regression. There is, after all, the writing of one's first play, first words, first letters. One need not write a play as a condition for writing another one, any more than one needs to have a toothache as a condition for having another one. The V_H thesis promises nothing if not originality! It confers on the actor precisely the status of an author and, accordingly, is not surprised or embarrassed when a "first work" or "novel twist" or "unexpected production" is forthcoming.

Part of the reigning confusion in the literature on human agency is attributable to a less than clear and consistent use of the term "action." Philosophers and psychologists have been far too beholden to examples from Physics and far too eager to keep even these unwisely chosen examples as simple as possible. Thus do we find a literature that is bloated with instances of raising one's arm, throwing a ball, lifting an object, scratching a nose. Indeed, most of the behavior chosen to illustrate this or that hypothesis is best regarded not as a species of *action* but as a species of *reaction* or reflex. The fallacy behind such choices is the belief that because human activity is part of a closed system in some of its expressions it is part of a closed system in all of them. The fallacy, then, is just another version of D_2.

A system is *closed* when all observable and measurable transactions are covered by principles of conservation; when an "output" from any part of the system is an "input" to the system as a whole; when all events have their effects only within the system and when events beyond the system have no effects on it; when, in a word, the "content" of the system is constant, no matter how varied the form of the content may be. We can, for example, make a strip out of two metals with different coefficients of expansion such that the strip bends in one direction when the surrounding temperature falls and in the other direction when it increases. A simple thermostat is thereby created with the strip closing an electrical circuit (and thus turning on the furnace) when the room is cool and opening the same circuit when the room is hot. Here we have a *closed system* which may not be different in principle from the "human system" when arms are raised, balls are thrown, objects are lifted, and noses are scratched. In all such instances we are dealing only with rudimentary ballistic responses that are defined in precise mechanical-mathematical terms. It is, however, just because such occurrences are so completely describable that we are lulled into the belief that invoking "agency" adds nothing. To see what "agency" adds we must turn to events whose mechanical properties are not the salient ones or to events even whose mechanical properties are not "mechanically" describable in an exhaustive way.

We need not choose Hamlet to illustrate the point. Consider only a virtuoso performance of, say, the Moonlight Sonata. The final movement of this piece taxes even the most accomplished pianist. There are stretches when a dozen or more notes must be struck within a second or so; i.e., when the interval between successive "actions" is far too short to allow the sensory consequences of action-1 to be delivered to the brain in time to influence the motor events that will lead to action-2. Clearly, what the virtuoso performer is doing is different from what a novice does even when the latter strikes two successive notes very (equally) quickly. The master of the piece, we say, has something of a "motor template" built into his system (brain?) such that, once the first note in a series is struck, the entire "template" is triggered and the remaining notes in the series are "read-out," as it were, without any deliberation on the part of the pianist. It would make no sense in such a case to refer to the striking of any given note as "intentional," but we would scarcely describe the performance as "accidental" or "unintended" or "unconscious." The "action" in such cases is the playing of the Sonata, and not the striking of individual keys. What we finally judge are the hours and years of preparation for this "action"; a preparation that culminates in so disciplined and so habitual a series of reactions as to yield a nearly perfect performance.

Suppose now that, when we insist the pianist is an "agent" whose achievements have been forged out of hope, desire, resolve, etc., we are asked by the Davidsonian, "Is there anything added to 'He played the Moonlight Sonata' by invoking the concept of him as an agent?" Or, "Was his causing the performance itself an action or was it just the performance itself?" Our answer will be unavoidably truncated. Indeed, "He played the *Moonlight* Sonata" so thoroughly entails the notion of "agency" that reference to "agency" is entirely gratuitous in such cases. Like "playing" chess, "playing" the piano with mastery is unimaginable with agency removed. There are, of course, player-pianos and even more modern gadgets by which musical compositions are "played" by no more than machinery, but this is quite beside the point. There are no equivalent instances of virtuouso performances of the *Moonlight* Sonata by *human beings* who have never studied, practiced, desired, believed, etc.

I dwell on this illustration because it brings into focus two important attributes of actions. The first is that, as habitual modes of behavior, some actions are neither "intentional" nor "unintended" and require as a different modifier the word *habitual* or its kin. We might think of these as "second-nature" actions which unfold with the same precision and predictability as (first-nature) reflexes. They are common in the performing arts and in other technical persuits, though on some philosophical accounts even virtue must become thus habitual! But what is important here is to recognize that an action need not stand in the same temporal relation with the intentions that produce it as (natural) effects stand in relation to their (natural) causes. The reason we are disinclined to describe the pianist's striking of each note as "intentional" or "unintended" is because we tend to adopt physical models when describing *reasons-actions* sequences. But the theory of human agency (V_H) rejects the applicability of just these models and is not, therefore, to be charged with queerness or eccentricity when requiring or affirming temporal relations unheard of in the physical realm. The actor is the agent behind his habits not in the sense that a cause stands behind its effects but in the sense that Shakespeare is the author of *Hamlet*; i.e., in the sense of personal creation.

The second attribute of actions illustrated by the virtuoso performance is that they must be *intelligible* in the way that cause-effect sequences are not. Berkeley was getting at just this point when he chided that he could find nothing in the gravitational laws except the effects themselves. We claim to know that

A and B are causally related when A and B have a common history in our experiences. We do not impose the criterion of *intelligibility* on the causal relation. For example, we do not say that it somehow makes more sense that short-wavelength radiation yields the experience of blue whereas longer wavelengths yield that of orange and red. After all, the particular relationship between energy and color vision could have been otherwise and we would have had no grounds for being surprised had it been so. But what makes a sample of human behavior an *action* is its connection to real or imaginable goals in the future and to occurrent beliefs and preparations in the past.

We have, then, several grounds on which to base objections to the thesis that reasons are (or are somehow like, or function as) causes. First, the actions arising from reasons are not determined in the way that effects are determined by causes. The temporal relations between the former dyad are different from those obtaining between the latter. Nor are actions readily or aptly reducible (without remainder) to discrete, ballistic responses common to closed mechanical systems. In some cases, the "action" is an entire ensemble of events, no element of which is *intelligible* when removed from the ensemble in which it is otherwise and actually imbedded.

Some actions clearly have open-system attributes and must arise from agents who are open systems in this respect. We need consider only *information* as an example of an unbound variable not covered by principles of conservation and (thus) not explicable in the language of physical economies. We do not lose information by passing it on, nor does it get used up by being used, nor (as best as we can tell) do we need proportional amounts of energy to increase its extent. Even as the entropy of the universe increases, we—on our little solar satellite—decrease it locally with every successful imposition of order, predictability, and understanding.*

The psychological term we have customarily applied

---

*Note that recent cosmologies are more neutral on the monotonic increase in entropy, but not because of anything *we* are doing!

to cover all of this is "creativity," though the word has been devalued by inflationary usage. But what the word is getting at is often neglected by those who would attempt to abosrb human actions into the causal nexus in which (merely) physical transactions occur. Perhaps "agency," too, has become so colored by spiritistic innunendo as to disturb the repose of the nonsectarians! Yet, the infelicitousness of a word cannot justify a denial of the facts the word seeks to define or depict or explain. To those who wonder what we've added to or learned about an event when we say that Smith, as an intending agent, brought it about, we can say that we've added *understanding* to what would otherwise have been an unintelligible and bald perception. As it happens, "Smith was the intending agent who brought about X," is *not* shorthand for "Smith X'ed." It is a radically different claim, even if flawed or misguided. The former sentence carries with it what is ultimately a *moral* assignation that is inapplicable in principle to any and every purely natural event (effect). It carries with it also a recognition (perhaps faulty or misguided) that the event thus brought about had a *point*, whereas purely natural events (effects) do not. (It never makes sense to ask what is the point of Ohm's Law).

As should be clear, concepts of "agency" and "creativity" successfully dodge the problem of infinite regression by conferring on the actor the powers of authorship and originality, not to mention spontaneity, inconsistency, hesitation, and retreat. Being an agent is not, in itself, to perform an action but to frame an action-consequence sequence. Thus, being an agent—if there is an infinite regress involved at all—is to be an agent! And to *frame* an action-consequence sequence is not necessarily to realize it. The totally paralyzed patient is no less an agent for his incapacities, though he must be an unrequited one. There is a customary connection between agency and action, but not a logical one or, for that matter, a relentless psychological one.

We are left, therefore, with only one difficult question for V_H, and that is the nature of the relationship between agency and action, now that we have recognized that it is not the concept of agency itself that is troubled or in trouble. Just how is it wardly the striking of any given note as "intended" or as "unintentional," though we have no doubt but that the *action* of "playing the Moonlight Sonata" is intentional. Again, we can conceive of a performance—an *action*—none of whose constituents is "intended" (in the usual sense) but all of them collectively yielding an intended outcome. It is because of this that attempts to analyze actions into molecular or atomic components is useless and misleading labor if the goal is to understand the actions themselves. Properly regarded, what I have called "second-nature" actions are really *reactions* (reflex-like habits) amenable to a causal analysis and even a physiological or neural reduction. What stands behind actions are intentions and beliefs in addition to a competence gained by practice and preparation. What stands behind actions, that is, are *agents* framing action-consequence sequences. The realization of a given consequence requires typically not only additional actions but a number of reactions or responses or "behavioral elements," some or even most of which may not be—or may not continue to be—"intended" in the received sense. Where D_2 gains its ostensible strength is in the choice of these intermediary responses and in the ability to explain them in purely naturalistic-causal fashion. Where V_H suffers its ostensible losses is in often not being able to point to any particular "behavioral element" as one arising from an agent with the freedom to choose a course of action. Commonly, the defender of V_H, faced with an example like that of the pianist, wants to say that the pianist, as agent, intends to strike each note, but also does not know how to address the fact that so rapid a sequence of responses leaves no time for deliberation and choice. But the performance of the Moonlight Sonata is, in fact, a *remote consequence* of the agent's framing of action-consequence sequences. The actions relevant to this particular consequence—this particular performance—may be weeks or months or even years removed from the consequence itself. A useful analogy is the writing of a will: Smith's action (writing the will) made Jones a millionaire twenty years after Smith's action; i.e., once Smith had died and his will had been probated. What Smith intended to bring about was Jones's ultimate wealth and he employed the instrument of a will to accomplish it. It is

just in the nature of genuine actions that their intended consequences are often temporally remote and where the appearance
of a neat causal chain is largely illusory. The actor-agent who frames
action-consequence sequences does so without being able to "limit
possibilities" in the way that *bona fide* causes do. Thus, even in the
sense that such an agent does "cause" certain consequences, he
does not do so in the manner in which natural causes produce
natural effects. Indeed, on those occasions when he seems to do
so, it is only because his actions have availed themselves of natural causes. Smith puts rat poison in the basement and awakens
to discover a dead rat. The sense in which Smith caused the death
of the rat is different from the sense in which the poison caused
the death of the rat. Smith's action could not foreordain the efficacy of the poison, the rat's eating it or the rat's eating enough
of it for the outcome to be fatal. We see again that reasons are
not a species of cause and neither, therefore, are the actions arising from these reasons. In realizing or attempting to realize a given
consequence, agents take recourse to actions consistent with and
exploitative of the causal laws of nature, but distinct from them.

It is just this ontological gap between reasons and
causes that prohibits natural causes from determining *bona fide*
reasons. Natural causes can and do operate on the purely natural
(physical) conditions of the body such that Smith may be *caused*
(determined) to misperceive, miss the mark, fail to hear the cry
for help, see the wrong face in the crowd, forget his aunt's birth-
day, etc. It is in this way that he may be *caused* (determined) to
initiate or frame a nugatory action-consequence sequence or otherwise be "doomed to fail." Similarly, he may be distracted by pain,
weakened by hunger or blinded by emotion. In many and various
ways the particular action-consequence sequence framed by an
agent may reflect conditions that are themselves not part of the
sequence, not intended by the agent, and still causally involved
in the process of framing such a sequence. It may even be the
case that, in light of the ubiquity of such natural influences, there
is never an instance of an utterly *authentic* intention, desire, belief
or plan. That is, practically it may be the case that such so-called
propositional attitudes invariably rise only to the level of relative

fore, cannot incorporate them into action-consequence sequences.[38] Such motives cannot "cause" any part of *Wealth of Nations* that Smith caused *as an agent*. The type-3 explanation also
fails since, to train (reinforce, "shape," "brainwash," encourage,
exhort) Smith to do X, there must be an envisaged X to begin
with. It makes some sense to say that Smith was reinforced to
write, but surely not to say that he was reinforced to write *Wealth
of Nations!* This same criticism applies of course to type-9 explanations, as it does to types 4 and 6. The action we have set out
to explain has *Wealth of Nations* as its specific consequence and it
cannot therefore be explained by any general condition of mental
health or life's circumstances. And, finally, explanation-types 5, 7
and 8 are merely circumlocutions. What, after all, do we mean by
"Smith wrote *Wealth of Nations*" if not that he had the *requisite* personality, intelligence, motivation, etc?

These nine explanation-types all fail individually and
collectively to explain *Wealth of Nations,* but each does figure in one
or another form in any complete explanation we might attempt
to fashion. Properly framed, they constitute the overall psychological and social context within which Adam Smith's authentic
intentions to write just what he wrote must be realized. We may
go so far as to say that the action-consequence sequence culmi-
nating in *Wealth of Nations* could not have been realized had such
conditions as those embraced by 1–9 not prevailed. Understood
in this way, such conditions may be taken to be *permissive* rather
than determinative. The conditions of Smith's brain and body, the
environment of his childhood, and the many other factors over
which Smith could not exercise intentional control, make up the
totality of that causal context within which possibilities are limited and within which also a given action-consequence sequence
must strive for achievement. This sort of "soft determinism" is,
indeed, compatible with V_H and with common sense. But it does
not challenge the concept of *agency* or even address it. Alas, it assumes it! Just what is it that such conditions limit—just what
possibilities do they allow or withhold—if not the accomplishments envisaged by the framer of an action-consequence se-

quence? Such conditions are permissive but not determinative of actions and thus they are not the causes of them.

Volition and Motivation

The ageless excuse for incontinent actions is "The spirit is willing but the flesh is weak," an excuse that often is regarded as a challenge to the alleged freedom of the will itself. We retain the ancient Greek word *akrasia* to cover those instances in which a person has failed to do what he judges to be the right thing to do, even though there is no external and constraining imposition. We turn again to Donald Davidson for a most economical statement of the dilemma created by what we usually regard as incontinent actions:

> P_1. If an agent wants to do x more than he wants to do y and believes himself free to do either x or y, then he will intentionally do x if he does either x or y intentionally. The second principle connects judgements of what it is better to do with motivation or wanting:
> P_2. If an agent judges that it would be better to do x than to do y, then he wants to do x more than he wants to do y. P_1 and P_2 together obviously entail that if an agent judges that it would be better for him to do x than to do y, and he believes himself to be free to do either x or y, then he will intentionally do x if he does either x or y intentionally. This conclusion, I suggest, appears to show that it is false that:
> P_3. There are incontinent actions.[39]

In addressing the general question of *How Is Weakness of the Will Possible?* from which the foregoing passage is taken, Davidson is drawn to the conclusion that, in the matter of incontinence, "the actor cannot understand himself: he recognizes, in his own intentional behavior, something essentially surd,"[40] since there can be no rational basis for choosing to act when, by one's own lights, a different and better course of action is freely available. Thus, as Davidson notes, there is no point in inquiring as to the reason for such an action for "the agent has no reason."[41] Here I shall not review Davidson's argument for this conclusion—interesting and, in my view, sound though it is. Rather, let us take these passages from his essay as a point of entry to the larger question of the relationship between motives and intentions and the bearing this relationship has on the question of free will and on the proposition that human agency stands behind human actions.

We may begin by noticing that the predicates in Davidson's P_1 and P_2 are of a radically different psychological nature, "wanting" and "judging" having no more in common than "needing" and "affirming." Accordingly, it is not at all difficult to imagine someone wanting to do x more than y while recognizing that y is better (more prudent, more noble, more lawful) than x. The ordinary way of distinguishing between wants and judgments is to regard the former as arising from emotional and motivational ("visceral") factors, whereas the latter are taken to be grounded in cognitive and rational ("cerebral") processes. But just where the *will* stands in all of this is not clear. Taken as a whole, the modern psychological literature makes virtually no distinction between motivated and willed behavior, except to refer to the latter as little as possible or to treat it as a hoary metaphysical notion bequeathed by the Schoolmen. But we must now begin to wonder whether the ancient practice—still common in psychological and philosophical discourse—of partitioning persons into congeries of "faculties," "motives," "volitions," and "judgments" is the most useful way to comprehend the relationship between agents and their actions. At a common-sense level, persons generally conduct themselves in a manner likely to bring about a certain state of affairs. Some such states answer to the general description "health" or "freedom from suffering"; but there are other states that do not make any apparent contact with the needs of the body as such.

Now, to bring about a state of affairs is, minimally, to have some conception of what that state is, and how it differs from the prevailing one. This is all the work of rationality and is inexplicable in motivational or "visceral" terms. The creature that consumes food *so that* a given state of affairs will be thereby produced is an agent; the one that behaves similarly, but with no such pictured or framed state of affairs thus conceived, is not. Surely many animals achieve by instinct what human beings can accomplish only through deliberation. Take the case of someone marooned and having access either to water or to food, but not to both, though having good reason to expect a change in his fortune if he can hold on long enough. Quite apart from the psychobiological question of whether his desire for food is greater or less than his desire for water, the stranded party who *knows* that he can live longer without food than without water will engage in deliberations unavailable to a mere creature similarly situated. Thus, even if the stranded man unwisely answers to his desire for food, he will do so *unwisely*. A complete description of his intentions will, therefore, require attributions that would be inapplicable to a similarly behaving brute or person ignorant of the relative costs of unrequited hungers and thirsts.

The very expression "weakness of the will" is misleading. In some respects, so is "freedom of the will." Less confusion would surround the entire issue if we agreed to treat persons as "agents" in the sense that on at least some occasions their behavior can be explained only as an expression of a framed action-consequence sequence where the consequence was intentionally selected by the agent. We will not find ourselves hearing that he "chose to bring it about against (his own) better counsel," though we will often discover that he failed to do what the framed sequence required if the consequence was to have any likelihood of occurring.

The person who "acts on impulse" is better regarded as *reacting*. He has not grounded his conduct in reasonableness and thus his behavior—even if it leads to a desired state of affairs—could not have arisen from the *framing* of such. Unlike Davidson, I would not be inclined to think of such behavior as *intentional*, though I would regard as intentional the readiness to abandon reason and to react to the impulses. What is ultimately an incontinent action is one that allows permissive conditions to be causally determinative. The incontinent action thus arises from a cause rather than a reason in settings in which the actor, through reason, could have prevented permissive conditions from becoming causally efficacious. The actor has "thrown in the towel"—and has done so *intentionally*—so that his subsequent behavior can in fact be spared the moral burden carried by genuine actions. The man who is floating in the ocean does not intend to move where the tides take him, but he may be held responsible for placing himself in a situation in which purely natural occurrences would dictate his subsequent behavior.

It seem clear, then, that the psychology of motivation has little or nothing to do with V_H, since volitions are essentially cognitive affairs. Prevailing motives, as noted in the previous section, provide part of the general context within which action-consequence sequences are framed. They constitute some of the conditions the agent must weigh or oppose or exploit, but they are not determinative of actions since they are not sources or attributes of reasons. Considered as "drives" or as biological conditions of disequilibrium or need, motives represent conditions that wax and wane; conditions that can be satisfied and thus eliminated. Few of the significant human desires are of this sort. The actor-agent who would bring about consequences that are just or fair, or who would seek to honor and preserve friendship, or who would have his conduct relate intelligibly to his desires, is not someone who gets enough of all this and then turns to something else! Needs and wants can be sated in a way that the *desires of reason* cannot.

Perhaps what V_H should be construed as asserting is not freedom of the "will"—whatever that refers to—but the power to represent freely or depict or frame intelligible connections between actions of a certain kind and states of affairs that preserve this very power. Like any power, and unlike any cause, this one too can be withheld intentionally or abused or neglected. Note, then, that it is entirely unlike hunger, thirst, pain, and those other "motivating" conditions that impel palliating behaviors or those ordinarily thought of as "drive-reducing." These are part of the person as a *closed* system. The freedom customarily ascribed to the will is better construed as a set of initiatives the actor-agent can take to escape from this closed system, if only in his intended (as opposed to realized) objectives.

In referring to the *desires of reason* I may seem to be mixing apples and oranges, but I can find no other phrase that better expresses the widespread (universal?) penchant for making our actions intelligible, or for the confusion and consternation resulting from irrational behavior on the part of others. Ascribing desires to rationality is odd only because of the historical habit of compartmentalizing psychological states as if they occupied different locations! Perception, cognition, desire, affect, and rationality are words we use when we wish to highlight one or another of the many concurrent performances or states associated with any significant action. As William James warned, however, it is only by way of the "psychologist's fallacy" that we come to regard the actor himself as divisible into the sorts of processes and states which our experiments artificially extract from the whole. Lest we commit the same fallacy, we quickly acknowledge that the "desires of reason" are just the desires of a person when that person exercises his rationality for the purpose of choosing a course of action toward a (desired) goal. There is no "reason" external to the person or living as another entity within the person. To select rationality (or "cognitive processes") for study is a worthy undertaking but it is not to be thought of as akin to taking a specimen off a shelf. The latter action removes something from where it once was; selecting this or that "process" does not remove it from the person who possesses it, nor does it impersonalize it. It is still Smith's rationality, even if in the experiment it seems to operate the way everyone else's does. The researcher may understand such processes in a way that Smith doesn't. The experiment may make accessible to study all sorts of operations of which the subject is entirely unaware. But to this very extent the findings are unlikely to provide an explanation of Smith's actions, for to explain these we must include in the account Smith's reasons, intentions, desires—everything of which Smith *must* be conscious for his behavior to be properly regarded as an action in the first place.

Summary

Psychological explanations, striving for scientific status, are routinely phrased in causal language although theoretical psychologists remain insufficiently aware of the ambiguities surrounding the concept of causation even (especially) within the developed sciences. With due caution, however, we can regard a causal explanation in science as one that severely limits possible outcomes by asserting a law. Though we remain open on the question of whether causes *necessarily* yield their effects, we recognize that traditional arguments against necessitation are both unconvincing and at odds with at least the implicit understanding of the developed sciences. In any case, the Humean analysis of causation is seen to be defective and weak, offering finally no justification for attempts by psychologists to equate causal explanation with no more than reliable or even unfailing coincidences.

If contemporary understandings of causation are incomplete in Psychology, notions of "determinism" are often incoherent. Regarding the laws of science as descriptions of causal determination, we examine the application of such nomic principles to human actions and discover a variety of often striking incompatibilities. There is at least some human conduct that is explicable only in terms of *agency*, where an agent is taken as an entity able to frame action-consequence sequences intentionally and to harbor authentic motives, desires, and beliefs. We see that *hard* psychological determinism D_2 is far less plausible than hard voluntarism V_H, although the latter has been too loyal to ambiguous concepts of "free will." We have good reason to be skeptical about the reality of classifications that would sharply divide the human psychological domain into reason, emotion, motivation, belief, volition, etc. Agents (actors) are not "free" in the unqualified sense of suffering no condition of constraint or coercion imposed on their actions. Rather, through rational assessments of a given situation, persons are able to liberate their actions from natural-causal conditions that would otherwise be dispository. Absent rationality, these conditions are in fact causal; with rationality, they are best regarded as *permissive* or at least to some degree not binding or determinative. Properly understood, "freedom" is freedom from causal determination and is secured *only* by operations that are rational. The "will," therefore, is free only to the extent that volitions are taken to be *desires of reason* or rational desires rather than (brute) motives, inclinations, urges, and the like.

A species of "soft determinism" is thus coherent, or at least not self-contradictory, but only when applied to cases in which the rational capacities of the actor are either suspended or blunted or lacking. Typically, variations in these capacities are continuous rather than discrete and thus any given sample of significant behavior may well include both causally determined and "free" features. This is especially obvious in instances of "second-nature" actions—habitual forms of behavior that are the consequence of a (perhaps long ago) framed *action-consequence sequence.*

None of the various explanatory schemes dominant within Psychology directly confronts or coherently includes the features of agency, authenticity, intentionality and related elements of V_H. Thus, none of these schemes describes, let alone explains, human actions.

CHAPTER THREE

Reductionism: Models, Metaphors and Similes

It is often alleged that models of complex processes or phenomena, no matter how lacking these are in face-validity, have *heuristic* value. By this is meant that the models are tools of discovery permitting conceptual manipulations that would be impossible or impractical at realistic levels of observation and description. Commonly within Psychology the models are of this or that "system"—the nervous system (or parts thereof), motivational systems, memory systems—though the concept of a "system" is not clear at the outset. Indeed, it is not at all clear which criteria are adopted as psychologists set out to construct such models. If they have anything in common it is the property of relative simplicity. The actual processes or phenomena are said to be "reducible" to a simpler model of them or somehow explicable in the simplified (reduced) language permitted by the model. In this chapter we shall inquire into the heuristic contributions made by various reductionistic strategies and the usefulness of explanations arising from them. Some classification at the outset will be helpful. What is a model and what distinctions should be made among the different types?

Analytical and Physical Models

It is not enough to say that, for example, X is a model of Y to the extent that X has properties in common with properties of Y. This is too general and would permit very nearly anything to be a model of very nearly anything else. Rather, we say that X is a model of Y when those properties that permit Y to be assigned to a class or category (of things, processes, performances) are partially or fully preserved by properties of X. Where the preservation is secured through one or another form of *description*, the model is *analytical*. Where the preservation is secured through a mimicry of actual processes or performances, the model is *physical*. It is sometimes the case that analytical models are developed where the creation of physical models would be impossible; and it is sometimes the case that high-fidelity simulations (physical models) can be produced where no adequate analytical model is available. Thus, we can make reasonably good speech-synthesizers although we do not have adequate analytical models of the speech-producing mechanisms and processes of human beings. Similarly, we have detailed analytical models of quantum-phenomena that we are unable to simulate physically.

Understood in a certain light, the laws of science are universalized analytical models—typically, *mathematical* models—which describe observed causal sequences. The laws are *redescriptions* of things and events otherwise described in observation-language or, as we say, "empirically." What the mathematical model or "law" achieves is a kind of translation of observation terms into quantitative terms, the latter permitting accuracy and predictability not as readily achieved by the former.

As noted in the preceding chapter, Berkeley contended that Newton's celebrated law was *merely* a description of the observed effects themselves. Berkeley is not alone in wondering whether the laws of science ever rise higher than the level of translation or redescription. Are analytical models and the very laws of science nothing more than curve-fitting operations? If we already have the effects at the level of observation, what is gained (other than a certain economy) by putting them in the form of an equation? There is no point in striving for a *redescription* unless the existing descriptions are inadequate or defective; but if they are then any analytical model of them will (must) include the same inadequacies or defects as well! Such considerations have often encouraged commentators to be skeptical about the value of analytical models.[1] But the criticism itself is based on an incomplete recognition of both the nature and the purpose of analytical models, not to mention a certain innocence about the nature of observation itself.

Illustratively, we might examine the well-known psychophysical law according to which the magnitude of a sensation—say, the sensation of brightness—is a linear function of the intensity of the visual stimulus when this is expressed in logarithmic units. Thus,

$$(1)\ B = k\ \log_{10} I\ \text{(Fechner's Law)}$$

Now, to the critic who insists that (1) provides only a summary of what we already know, we are obliged to inquire into just what it was we "knew" prior to articulating this particular law. If what the critic means is that the actual brightness-estimations at various levels of intensity were all a matter of record, this of course is true. But the very act of measuring sensation-magnitudes against systematically altered intensities of stimulation proceeds from a model of the sort given in (1). That is, the model—though in less than complete form—is already in place, as it were, when the experimental program is undertaken. The model that generates the research is of the form,

$$(2)\ B = f(I)$$

and the whole point of the experiment is to establish the precise function of intensity that brightness is. Note that the actual sequence of events is not RESEARCH$\longrightarrow$ (2)$\longrightarrow$ (1), but (2)$\longrightarrow$ RESEARCH$\longrightarrow$ (1).

Because of this, it is only partly correct to say (as Berkeley did) that the analytical model simply describes (or redescribes) already possessed knowledge. A scientific law is not simply a redescription of data but a refinement of an earlier (and perhaps only implicit) law which itself was not a description but a conceptualization of nature. It is precisely because analytical models are conceptualizations and not merely summaries of fact that they are productive and not merely descriptive of nature. This point is illustrated by the same example. Begining with (2), we proceed to conduct inquiries that culminate in (1) where the values of B are based upon responses by the experimental subject. Now knowing that, at the level of "experience," the relationship between B and I is logarithmic, we can ask where in the system as-a-whole this log-transformation takes place.[2] Indeed, an entire program of research is organized around such questions as:

Is (1) invariant across different values of stimulus duration?
How is (1) affected when different wavelengths of stimulation are used?
Does (1) depend upon the size of a stimulus or its retinal locus?
Is (1) preserved in the behavior of the receptors?
Is (1) preserved in the responses of optic nerve fibers?
Do gross cortical recordings yield (1)?

We see, then, that far from merely describing a given set of data-points, the analytical model—here, the psychophysical law—generates and directs any number of experiments leading to discoveries otherwise ignored by any purely descriptive account.

There are dangers as well as profound implications contained in the otherwise harmless equal sign. Expressions of the sort,

$$(3) \quad E = mc^2$$

are quite different from (1) and (2) in that something radically different from a functional relationship is conveyed. In (3), the $=$ expresses an *identity* relation such that matter and energy are but different manifestations of each other. With (3), what has been achieved is a genuine *reduction* in that we are no longer required to partition nature into entirely distinct ontological categories, one containing only matter and the other containing only energy.

In both (1) and (2), however, there is no such ontological reduction, since in neither equation does the $=$ stand for IS

IDENTICAL TO or IS THE SAME AS. What (1) and (2) provide are *transfer functions* allowing us to specify the value of B once we have chosen values of I. What is asserted in (1) or (2) is not that brightness *is* I or $\log_{10}$I, but that it is a *function* thereof. Too often analytical models are taken as reductive when they are only functional, and the illusions of reductionism thus become pervasive. Again, the psychophysical law helps to clarify these important considerations. We know, for example, that brightness-estimates are entirely independent of the duration of flashes when durations are very brief. The well-known reciprocity law of Bloch establishes the temporal limit at about 100 milliseconds for small stimuli delivered to the fovea. Thus, with such stimuli, (1) can be modified as follows:

$$(4)\ B = k\log_{10} E\ (\text{under } C_1)$$

where E is the total *energy* in a flash and where C_1 refers to those conditions in which flashes are foveally delivered and subtend angles of less than 1° on the retina. Now, if we take (1) as actually asserting,

$$(5)\ B = k\log_{10} I \times t\ (\text{where } t \text{ is duration})$$

then (4) is a successful *reduction* of (1) in that, under C_1, it permits the elimination of at least one ontological category; *viz.*, time. It is *not*, however, a reduction B and is thus not even relevant to the issue of reductionistic *psychology*. Given that expressions such as those of (1), (2), (4), and (5) are unlike (3)—given, that is, that they are not identity-relations but transfer-functions—no operation performed on the physical side of the = *can* affect the psychological part of the expression in any way whatever. We might alter the physical side in any number of ways, since the total energy in the flash will depend upon the intensity, the area of the radiating source, the wavelength and duration of light, the density of the media through which the light passes, etc. But these considerations have no bearing, finally, on arguments for a reductionistic psychology—or a reductive model of perception—because they in no way affect the boundaries of the ontological domain in which the sensation of brightness is found. Again, a successful and bona fide reduction is achieved only when we succeed in showing that what were once thought to be functional relationships are, in fact, identity-relationships of the kind expressed in (3).

It may be argued that I have so far confined the meaning of "reduction" to the number of terms in the analytical model and have ignored the nature of the terms. One might say, for example, that if (1) is true and if, further, we discover that,

(6) $B = f(D_n)$,
where D_n are discharge-rates of neurons

and, finally, that

(7) $D_n = k\log_{10} I$

then we have *reduced* the sensation of brightness to D_n by establishing the equivalence of (1) and (7). This, however, is fallacious, for all we have now accomplished is the discovery that one of the ways (1) comes about is by way of (7). What (7) provides is not a *reduction* of (1) but one of its *explanations*. There is no alteration in our conception of "brightness"; only in our appreciation of some of the (neural) conditions associated with it or even necessary for it.

Where physical models are involved—simulations of one sort or another—the claims of reductionism are even further misplaced, though for reasons that are not widely noticed. In possession of, say, (1), (6) and (7) above, an engineer might set about to construct a device that responds to incident radiation in the visible region of the spectrum. The response might even be vocal, but whatever it is the functional relationship given in (1) is completely preserved. (It is worth noting that Bloch's law is reasonably well preserved in the behavior of photographic emulsions exposed to pulses of light. The earliest reciprocity laws were, in fact, based upon just such chemical processes in photography.) But what a simulation of this sort yields is not a *reduction* of (1) to something ontologically simpler; it results instead to the *replacement* of (1) by an expression with exactly the same number of ontological categories:

(8) $R = k\log_{10} I$
(where R is the device's response)

The R in (8) may be further reduced to, for example, a simple circuit or to complex chemical equations, but this has no bearing on B in (1). The physical model goes as far it can only when a reduction of R in (8) is shown to be identical to a similar reduction of D_n in (7). The further step, involving proof of the identity of B in (1) and, e.g., D_n in (7), can never be made solely on the basis of the adequacy of (8). Put another way, the Turing-argument is grounded in a mistake.[3] Reduction and replacement are different operations and entail different assumptions and implications. The modern vacuum cleaner is not a "reductive model" of what housekeepers did in the nineteenth century, but a replacement of the housekeeper's behavior by a device arising from entirely different principles of operation, to say the least. And the hope or the strategy on which are based attempts at veritable clone-like physical models cannot successfully depend on reductionistic theses either. If the achievement is totally successful, we will have an entity or a device indistinguishable from the entity supplying us with (1), and thus, far from having *reduced* (1), we will simply have repetitions of it.

Models and the Criterion
of Publicity—Wittgenstein's Bequest

A persistent theme in reductionistic psychology is the need or, as it were, the right to base models entirely on the measurable, public *behavior* of persons or "organisms," even if the behavior itself is to be regarded as a sign or correlate of some internal state or event. The strategy comes about by default in that the investigator is said never to have direct access to the "private" states, processes, or events of the subject (observer; reporter; "behaver"). The reasoning here is sound as far as it goes, as long as the implicit inadequacies are not overlooked. A paradigmatic case is provided again by the various psychophysical relationships of the broad form,

$$R = f(S)$$

where some chosen response (R) is examined over a range of values of the precisely controlled stimulus (S). As C. H. Graham proposed years ago,[4] the basic question animating all psychophysical research is ultimately a question about the stimulus-range over which responses are invariant. To ask, then, whether Smith and Jones "see the *same* red" is to ask only whether their respective stimulus-response functions are essentially the same or different. The question, then, when properly conceived is not about "private experiences" but *publicly* verifiable measures of, e.g., "redness." In brief, to inquire into what an observer perceives is to establish the degree of covariation expressed by stimulus-properties and response-properties.

As noted above, this is not an approach that yields a *reduction*, but a substitution or replacement. The $R = f(S)$ relationship rests upon the (at least implicit) assumption that the chosen (R) is itself quantitatively interchangeable with the relevant perception and its various magnitudes or qualities. It only makes sense to work with $R = f(S)$ if there are good reasons for assuming that $R = f(P)$, where (P) refers to the actual perceptual event or experience. For example, it is well established that the perceived brightness of a flash is regulated by Bloch's law (*vide supra*) but that reaction time is determined by the intensity of a flash independently of the flash's duration; i.e., reaction time does not reflect the $I \times t$ reciprocity relations obtained when perceived brightness is directly assessed. In light of this, were we to choose reaction time as the "public" evidence of perceived brightness, the implicit assumption—$R = f(P)$—would be invalid at all exposure-durations less than about 100 milliseconds.

Note, therefore, that the apparently "objective" measures of overt behavior are themselves either dubious or invalid or arise from arguments or other data to the effect that the behavioral data faithfully reflect the experiential or "psychological" states that are too "private" for experimental purposes! Graham's formulation of the strategy is a contribution to methodology, not ontology and, as such, his formulation and all like it cannot be taken as supporting reductionistic claims. *Nothing is reduced* when behavior is chosen over introspection or when a "public" datum is substituted for a "private" experience.

A notion that has made much progress in philosophical circles in recent decades is that a successful reduction was achieved by Wittgenstein's searching analysis of so-called "private languages"; an analysis that produced the conclusion that such languages were simply impossible and that so-called private states or sensations were therefore chimerical. Regrettably this analysis is set forth in his *Philosophical Investigations*[5] in so epigrammatic a fashion as to render his arguments elusive. The secondary literature spawned by them is enough to reveal the wide interpretive terrain marked off by these incomplete and somewhat homiletic utterances.[6] Nevertheless, these utterances have been considerable in their influence and constitute a formidable challenge to any explanation in Psychology grounded in assumptions about the "privacy" of experience and the ability of a language to express such experience.

We begin to comprehend the nature of this challenge when we ask, with Wittgenstein, "How do words *refer* to sensations?" (#243).[7] He raises this question after posing a case in which a person, in isolation, writes down or vocalizes something that somehow stands for each feeling or mood or sensation. What this would seem to yield is a "private language" whose terms are correlated with these "private experiences."

> The individual words of this language are to refer to what can only be known to the person speaking; to his immediate private sensations. So another person cannot understand the language. (#243)[8]

But if this is granted, we come to face to face with Wittgenstein's famous "beetle in the box" dilemma:

> Suppose everyone had a box with something in it: we call it a "beetle." No one can look into anyone else's box, and everyone says he knows what a beetle is only by looking at *his* beetle.—Here it would be quite possible for everyone to have something differ-

ent in his box. One might even imagine such a thing constantly changing.—But suppose the word "beetle" had a use in these people's language?—If so it would not be used as the name of a thing. The thing in the box has no place in the language-game at all; not even as *a something*; for the box might even be empty.—No, one can "divide through" by the thing in the box; it cancels out, whatever it is. (#293)[9]

However, to those who would take this passage as a vindication of radical behaviorism, Wittgenstein also makes clear that his analysis is not ontological but linguistic:

Are you not really a behaviourist in disguise? Aren't you at bottom really saying that everything except human behaviour is a fiction?"—If I do speak of a fiction, then it is of a *grammatical* fiction. (#307)[10]

It is central to Wittgenstein's philosophy that language is an irreducibly *social* affair. It is governed by rules and, as such, is conventional. But convention entails *social* standards. It is therefore oxymoronic to speak of a "private language" if, by this expression, one has in mind a language that is *in principle* knowable only to one person. Thus, when it comes to feelings or pains or sensations of any kind, it is entirely unclear that the terms used can in any way be *referential* if the conditions or states are in principle and totally "private." If Smith's "beetle" is changing while Jones's isn't and while Brown's box is actually empty, then their respective utterances of "beetle" are nonreferential. Quite apart from the ontological question of whether or not there is anything in any of these purely personal boxes, the utterances are *grammatical* fictions. The pain-words we come to employ once we have learned the "language game" do not therefore *describe* a private state but *replace* older and public expressions such as tears, crying, and grimaces.[11] Where Smith, as a child, once held his swollen cheek and sobbed, he now exclaims, "I have an intense toothache." If there is a grammatical reference in such an expression, it is the early class of public behaviors that have now been replaced by these words. It is because, as other players of the language-game, we know that "You have a toothache" (always in the past) referred to cheek-holding and crying-behavior, that we now can assign meaning to Smith's utterance, "I have an intense toothache." If the words were invented by Smith to refer only to *his* "beetle", no one—not even Smith—could extract a *conventional* reference from the utterance.

To accept this analysis is to adopt at least a *methodological* behaviorism and to grant to instrospective reports no psychological significance beyond the act of reporting. Graham's position is wed to this. The psychophysical experiment, accordingly, is not an inquiry into (private) sensations or perceptions as such, but a specification of the stimulus-range over which a given response (including a verbal report) remains invariant. As Graham himself was wont to say informally, psychophysical research is the study of, for example, "vision," not "seeing."

Wittgenstein was, himself, unable to stretch his analysis to cover the more fundamental ontological question as to the status of sensations. But even his modest objective—that of consigning "private language" to the category of grammatical fictions—was not achieved as fully as many of his disciples insist. It is not at all clear, for example, that anyone can learn the language-game—as it pertains to sensations—in the way that Wittgenstein envisaged. It makes good sense to say that Smith has violated linguistic conventions; that he has made a mistake or committed a "Freudian slip" or is guilty of a Spoonerism. But what sense does it make to say that Smith is similarly mistaken about his pain? I refer here not to the so-called *incorrigibility thesis*[12] to be discussed later but to the problem of *teaching* the language-game as Wittgenstein requires. The community of linguists who would shape the young and render them fit for participation can do so only by correcting mistaken uses. Thus, if Tommy says (incorrectly), "This is a knife," we can supply the corrective; "No, that is a spoon." The corrective is possible only if each such noun is ostensively defined. But suppose Tommy comes in clutching his stomach, crying, and declaring, "I have a toothache!" If we reply, "No, it must be a stomach ache because you're holding your stomach," we have not corrected Tommy's ache but his vocabulary or, more technically, his knowledge of human anatomy. Tommy has learned nothing new about his sensations; only about how to signal them and their location to others. He is learning how to answer the question, "Where does it hurt?"

Wittgenstein was dubious about claims of the sort, "No one can have *my* pains."

> Which are *my* pains? . . . In so far as it makes *sense* to say that my pain is the same as his, it is also possible for us both to have the same pain. And it would also be imaginable for two people to feel pain in the same—not just the corresponding—place. That might be the case with Siamese twins, for instance. (#253)[13]

But this has no bearing finally on the existential fact of *this* person's pain, for every pain is *someone's* pain. Even granting that Siamese twins could have pains in the same place there would still be *two* pains felt and not one. From the fact or allegation that, "it is also possible for us both to have the same pain," it does not follow that there is only one pain, nor does it follow that a person who has the same pain as I do therefore has *my* pain. It would, after all, not follow from the fact that someone has the same memory of an event that I do that that person has *my* memory.

Wittgenstein wondered about just what the "criterion of identity" (#253) is in such instances and, although this is an interesting question, it may well be beside the point at issue. A given pain—say, a toothache—has minimally the attributes of duration, location, and intensity. These might be taken as the criteria of *sameness* in that, if Smith and Jones have pains of identical duration and intensity occurring in their respective left-incisors, the pains answer to identical descriptions. Nonetheless, we still have *two* pains, no matter how similar they might be in their prothetic and topographic properties. Alas, there can be no "criterion of identity" across percipients; only a "criterion of sameness." For there to be an identity it would be necessary that the pains or pain-descriptions be interchangeable and indiscernible, a condition that cannot be satisfied as long as we have two distinguishable percipients.

As noted, Wittgenstein was concerned chiefly with the grammatical dilemmas arising out of the notion of a "private" language developed to describe or refer to forever "private" sensations. He was quite aware of the fact that we inform others and are informed by them about all sorts of sensations, so he was surely not skeptical toward either the existence or the publicity of these sensations. The pivotal question in his analysis is the question of *reference.* Sensation-terms are either referential or are meaningless. If they are drawn from an irreducibly private vocabulary, they are removed from all possible language-games and are therefore unintelligible even to the user. But since such terms are intelligible, their referents must be public. Thus, sensation-terms derive their meaning from the ensembles of behavior to which they were initially attached and which, in time, they come to replace. So far so good. But from a psychological (in contrast with a lexical or philosophical) perspective, we are still left with the task of determining of what this behavior itself is (was) a function. The psychological analysis cannot stop with the observation that talk of a certain kind has come to replace some other kind of behavior. We must press on to establish the original, $R = f(S)$, if our ultimate psychological explanations of verbal R's are to make any contact with reality.

Whatever the final standing may be of Wittgenstein's conceptual analysis, it appears to be defective beyond repair as a psychological account of sensations. There is certainly no empirical evidence to support the supposition that congenital mutism leads to life-long patterns of infantile modes of pain-induced behavior. This may seem to be a trivialization of a profound philosophical conjecture but, as I noted in the first chapter, the philosopher who would instruct psychologists might at least occasionally consult the realms of fact to make sure that his assumptions have not already been overcome by the data. The patient in intractable pain, undergoing a thalamotomy for the relief of this pain, is consulted by the surgeon to signal when the sensation is attenuated. Obviously rule-governed conventions must be observed by patient and doctor if the (public) behavior of the patient is to be regarded as revealing the (private) sensation that the surgery is to eliminate. But to engage in the convention the patient must have something with which to correlate his own behavior. The patient must have the pain! And in raising his hand to signal something like "it's less severe now," the patient is not *replacing* but in fact is *describing* the sensation. The affair is not much different from a game in which one of the players is to raise his hand when he has the solution to a mathematics problem. The solution is "his" and remains utterly private until he voices it. We don't know whether or not he has solved the problem until he publicizes what he knows, but *he* knows whether he tells us or not. Suppose, now, that there are five such players and all of them raise their hands at just the same time. Let us suppose further that all give exactly the same solution to the problem. Shall we ask with Wittgenstein what is to be the criterion of identity in such cases? What difference would it make if the root question has to do with the privacy of mental events or, better, with the private *ownership* of one's ideas?

It is true, but only trivially, that psychological research into mental or sensory processes must avail itself of response-indicators of the cognitive or perceptual events of interest. The response-indicators provide the only basis upon which the investigator *can* know that the experimental subject has experienced or cognized anything. But these indicators, to the extent that they are valid, are not to be regarded as elements of a *reductive* analysis for, again, nothing has been *reduced*. Indeed, to the extent that the response-indicator provides only a partial record of what the subject has actually experienced or cognized, the reduction is achieved at the cost of validity. What the properly conducted psychophysical or cognitive study strives for is a narrowing of the response-domain such that variation across subjects will not be increased by sources of variance intrinsic to the response-indicators themselves. (We would not have subjects heft a forty-pound weight in a reaction-time study, for example, nor in a color-naming study do we usually permit "azure," "beige," "vermillion," and the like.) But in reducing the range of permissible responses the experimenter also reduces the number of stimulus-variables governing these responses. In the end, it is not the "mental" that has been reduced to something nonmental or (somehow) less mental. It is the sample of mental events that has been artificially constricted for purposes of quantitative description. The use of public criteria is demanded by the very nature of research. But the assumption that these criteria are validly and consistently used by the percipient is necessary if the resulting data are to have any relevance at all.

In light of the foregoing, we are in a position to assess those models constructed out of a behavioristic perspective or one that treats only *output* variables in an attempt to simulate or mimic or "explain" psychological processes. The fallacy that is common to all of them is the assumption that systems displaying identical functional relationships—of the form $R = f(S)$—may be regarded as copies or clones of one another. The fact, of course, is that any given transfer-function can be materially produced in numerous and radically different ways. Consider only the number of different circuits or mechanical contrivances that will impose a logarithmic transformation on an input-signal. But, as noted at the beginning of this chapter, X is a *model* of Y only when those properties that permit Y to be assigned to a class or category are partially or fully preserved by properties of X. Let us take as an illustration the phenomenon of *selective forgetting* (Y) that is reliably associated with painful experiences. If the only memory-deficits that count as instances of Y are those empirically tied to painful experiences known to have been endured by the subjects under study, then "painful experiences" become conditional properties by which a given performance is assigned to the category Y. If we now construct a device—some sort of computer—whose memory-locations are cleared whenever an entry is followed by, say, an input-signal in excess of so many volts, we might conceivably produce a record of input-output relations exactly like the record produced by the experimental subjects. Is this a model? Is the "overvolting" of a circuit a "painful experience"? The conditional property required for assignment to category Y is to be found nowhere among the attributes of this device. Accordingly, the device is not a model of *selective forgetting*, but an overly cumbersome way of copying empirically obtained curves. What has been modeled is not the phenomenon but the experiment.

We are not to make too much of the criterion of publicity. The psychologist's attitude toward it should be one of resignation and not reverence. We would all prefer to get into the mind and sensorium of the experimental subject, but we must be content with reaction time, judgments of brightness, X's on a page, evoked brain potentials, and the like. It has been tempting and all too reassuring for decades now to regard the Wittgensteinian analysis and others like it as a warrant for abandoning the mental. But any analysis that proves the nonexistence of private sensations, thoughts, and feelings is itself a candidate for demythologizing. In regarding the criterion of publicity as something of a necessary evil we will be more inclined to find and use response-indicators that tap the mental realm most directly and deeply, and less inclined to adopt dimensionless indicators which are unrealistically "objective."

The same is true of specious "models" forged out of unrealistic or marginally valid behavioral data. The right sort of model is constructed *after* the fundamental processes have been examined. It is not productive to anticipate the examination and it is utterly misleading to assume simplicity simply because only a simple model has been conjured. One example of the right sort of model is that developed by those working in the area of speech-synthesis and speech-recognition.[14] Models in this area are based upon the known harmonic analyses performed by structures in the inner ear and the known performance of listeners required to recognize speech sounds under a variety of acoustically relevant conditions. Here the psychophysical data and the biophysical processes have been exhaustively examined. Resulting models, both analytical and physical, represent all of the major functional operations performed by actual auditory systems. Accordingly, such models come to have explanatory power and come to provide convenient and instructive means by which to test hypotheses and construct ever more complete theories of acoustic information-processing. These models do not, of course, incorporate the *sensation* of hearing but those processes on which such sensations ultimately depend. My point is that we have many good models of what a good model is. It is one that respects the complexity—the reality—of the phenomena to be modeled and that draws direction from the already established principles responsible for these phenomena. The goal of the model-builder is not *reduction* but a kind of *portraiture*. Accordingly (and unlike Wittgenstein), the model-builder searches for criteria of sameness and not criteria of "identity." The model is a portrait, not a photograph. What is left out is not a reality the model-builder refuses to accept but those (ontologically) undoubted elements not essential to the creation of a high-fidelity portrait.

Jerry Fodor pointed out some years ago[15] that the so-called Turing-game is generally framed in such a way as to be either uninformative or question-begging—liabilities that are common to behavioristic models. It is not enough to say that a machine has successfully played such a game when its performance leaves judges doubtful as to whether a person or a machine provided answers to questions or solutions to problems. As Fodor insisted, it matters *how* the machine accomplishes this; it matters too that such a machine is still unable to perform any number of other and even trivially simple tasks well within the capabilities of any person. As Fodor put it,

> Turing would presumably have been dissatisfied with a device that could answer questions about how to boil water if it routinely put the kettle in the icebox when told to brew tea. (pp. 126–127)[16]

We are tempted to say of such failures that the device knows some things and not others, and that it need pass only one relevant test to be regarded as "intelligent" or "cognitive" or (more boldly) "conscious." Clinical neurology turns up any number of patients who, though unarguably conscious persons, do the equivalent of putting the kettle in the icebox; apraxics who, for example, can tell us anything we want to know about a jacket but cannot put one on. What counts, then, is not whether a Turing machine can do everything or even most things done by human beings within a given perceptual or cognitive context, but whether it does anything *in just the way* that human beings do that same thing. What Fodor erected as the relevant criterion was a *functional equivalence* between the machine-processes and the human cognitive (or perceptual) processes by which the respective outputs are governed.

This is a sound strategy but, as we shall see in the next two sections, one that is not easy to translate into nonarbitrary and practical programs of research and theory.

Functional Equivalence

We may take as the thesis of functional equivalence (F.E.) that X is a model of Y if and only if (a) the outputs of X and Y under relevantly comparable conditions are relevantly indistinguishable and (b) the processes or internal operations generating these outputs are functionally equivalent. However, the criterion (b) assumes that we possess a *taxonomy* of functions and that we know which items within this taxonomy are available to Y. The brutal fact is that we remain unable to test (b) until the entire program of cognitive psychology has been brought to a successful conclusion!

This, however, is not the only problem, for even where we have some evidence to the effect that a given cognitive performance arises from a specific process (e.g., addition) it is not clear just what a device would have to do for it to be regarded as doing the "equivalent" of addition. What is the criterion or standard or test of "equivalence"? The device might be constructed in such a way as to hold an electrical charge in its capacitors and, on a given signal, to have all the capacitors discharge into some other device that gives a readout of total volts. We can say that the final readout is the sum of all previously stored charges, but it would be merely metaphorical to say that the device had been engaged in *the process of addition* or was "doing" addition.

It is easier, of course, to establish nonequivalence even when we lack a fixed standard of equivalence. There are the so-called *calendar savants* who can give the day of the week on which any date falls—past, present, or future. Such persons will need no more time to state on which day of the week April 7, A.D. 204 fell than on which day August 11, 1996 will fall. From the empirical fact that performance here is nearly entirely independent of the range of dates covered by the ability, it follows that the performance is not the equivalent of thumbing through a file or scanning a table. A more common example is memorizing the multiplication tables as an alternative to doing multiplication by the process of successive addition. The person engaging in the latter process will require more time to answer "7 times 6" than to answer "4 times 6." Indeed, assuming the same time is devoted to each set of 6's to be added, the total time needed to obtain the result will be a linear function of the value of the multiplier. Thus, "10 times 6" will take twice as long as "5 times 6." Once we discover, therefore, that the time required to answer multiplication problems is unaffected by the value of the multiplier—within some given range of values of the multiplier—we can be sure that the process is not one of successive addition. If we know in such a case that a computer is programmed to provide solutions by successive addition we can say that the program is not a model of the process employed by the person. Even though the respective outputs are relevantly indistinguishable, there is not a functional equivalence between the respective internal operations generating these outputs. To choose just one more example, we note that it takes very little time for an observer to decide whether a string of letters forms a known word; e.g., *prillicarn*. If this judgment required the observer to consult that mental file in which every known word is stored, the judgment would take an indefinitely long time and would be a function of the size of the vocabulary of each of the observers in the study. Clearly, the facts establish that the process involved in classifying strings of letters as words or nonwords is not iterative. A computer program that produces the same discriminations, but that does so by comparing each candidate-string of letters with every word stored in memory, would not be the functional equivalent of the human process, whatever the latter turns out to be.

Still, we do not now have the necessary catalogue of human cognitive processes, nor have we developed nonarbitrary criteria of equivalence. Perhaps Köhler's principle of *isomorphism* comes as close to a precise criterion of equivalence as anything proposed by psychologists,[17] but it is applicable, if at all, only to a relatively modest range of psychological processes. According to the principle, for every specific percept there is a unique brain-process that is isomorphic with it. Note that the principle does not require something "circular" in the brain when the percipient sees a circle! The principle is more subtle even if the Gestalt psychologists have not fully developed it. What isomorphism asserts is this: For any phenomenal experience (E), there is a corresponding brain-event (B) such that a unique function (f) renders properties of E equivalent to properties of B. It is not clear, however, that the concept of isomorphism is applicable to nonphenomenal mental events such as those ordinarily regarded as "abstract." What pattern or attributes of B, for example, might be isomorphic with the concept of the square root of minus 1 or "the largest positive integer" or a "transcendental number" or the logical relation of formal necessity? Moreover, a successful table of isomorphic relations, like a successful table of functional equivalents of any sort, would not be *reductive* in the (ontologically) required sense. The device that matches the person, process for process and output for output, is not a reductive model of the person but a (functional) clone or copy. For each discernible and relevant human cognitive or perceptual process, the designers have installed a process in the device. There is no sense in which the achievement of this one-to-one correspondence can count as a *reduction*. But, "Ah!", some will say, "there *is* a reduction, for when it comes to the device we need not refer to anything 'psychological' or 'mental' or 'private' in accounting for its operations and its performance."

Not at all! The lexical economies are utterly illusory. Reference to or the creation of each of the device's processes implicitly revives the "psychological," for this is just what the process has been modeled after. One who is trained in Morse Code might just as well proclaim, "Ah! I no longer have to burden myself with the uselessly ornamented words of English, for now I can say everything using no more than dots and dashes." The plain fact is that Morse Code either allows every possible sentence in the coded language to be expressed—in which case there is no *reduction* of the language—or it eliminates sentences, in which case it is a defective code. To say that the works of Shakespeare can be "reduced" to a twenty-six-letter alphabet is false unless the proviso is that the letters can be combined in any possible sequence and set off from each other by marks of punctuation. But given this proviso, there has not been a "reduction" of the works of Shakespeare. Rather, the qualified statement establishes the set of *all possible literary works*! This set is larger than "the works of Shakespeare," not smaller.

Reductive Materialism

If there is to be a plausible and successful reductive model it is one likely to come from the neural or brain-sciences rather than from the various schools of behaviorism. No behavioristic thesis has successfully reduced the ontological domain of Psychology, or even made a good case for the equivalence of mental and behavioral variables. Whether or not Psychology can "get along just as well" without reference to inner life, consciousness, private mental states, etc. is a question of strategy, not ontology, and the force of the claim has little behind it except for the criterion of publicity considered in chapter 2.

Various forms of reductive materialism, however, are not just pragmatic or strategic programs, but genuinely ontological proposals. There is, for example, *eliminative materialism*, whose defenders insist that mental terms will be successively removed from the vocabulary as scientific findings come to show that, for each such term, there is a unique neural or physical event that exhaustively describes it.[18] Then, too, there is the kindred Identity Thesis[19] according to which every mental state or event is *in fact* a state or an event in the brain such that, to refer to the mental is invariably to refer only to such a neural event or state. Finally, there are garden-variety forms of *epiphenomenalism* which, though not *reductive* in the ontological sense, do challenge any theory that would confer special or private or transcendent status on mental life. In arguing that each identifiable mental event is uniquely de-

termined (caused) by an antecedent brain-process, the epiphenomenalist has not reduced the ontological realm of Psychology
but has reduced the size of the explanatory vocabulary needed to
account for psychological events.[20] What is common to all three
theses is the insistence that the brain (or, more generally, the
material organization of the body) is not merely a necessary condition for (allegedly) mental life, but is causally sufficient. (Having a tooth is a necessary condition for having tooth-decay but is
not causally sufficient for tooth-decay.)

There are many different ways of expressing these
several theses, but perhaps the most dramatic is in the form of
hypothesized brain-transplants. To wit: If Smith's living brain were
placed in the suddenly brain-dead but living body of Jones, all
true and relevant psychological attributes of Smith would thereupon be ascribable to Jones. Indeed, one philosopher endorsing
this view has gone so far as to say that, although this psychological transplantation may not be logically required, any alternative formulation would be "scientific nonsense."[21] In a word,
the psychological *self* goes where the brain goes. There is, then,
not really a "mind/body" problem but—if there is any problem at
all—a "mind/brain" problem; for it is the brain itself, and not any
other organ or system of the body, that constitutes the materially
causally sufficient condition for mental (or allegedly mental) events
(effects).

That the psychological *self* goes where the brain goes
has the ring of the obvious about it, but the proposition is not
without serious scientific liabilities. There is, as it happens, a body
functionally integrated with Smith's brain and not merely an ap-
pendage to it. Assuming that Smith has lived some years—long
enough at least for there to be a psychological "self"—his body
will have been modified by experiences, habits, diseases, and related influences. His peripheral nervous system will have taken
on certain properties uniquely tied to these influences. His au-
tonomic nervous system, to be sure, will have had its own con-
ditioning-history and will lend color and intensity and individu-
ality to the emotional events with which it comes to be associated.
It must be understood, therefore, that the brain that is moved to

a different body will, as a result, receive inputs from the periphery with characteristics determined by the nuances of these peripheral processes.

Without yet addressing the question of just what the psychological "self" is or how the concept of "self" is properly understood, we can still say that it is scarcely *nonsense* to have scientific reservations about the thesis under consideration. Smith's brain, just after the successful transplant, will be overcome by peripheral information of the strangest sort; odd odors, unfamiliar tactile sensations, peculiar visceral responses to various persons and places. Smith's brain will also initiate motor signals that will arrive at muscular and glandular destinations somewhat different in nature from those occupying Smith's original body. The resulting vocalizations will have a different sound; the digital precision once involved in piano playing may now be clumsy and tentative; a once learned second language may now be expressed in an utterly unintelligible way. To the extent that Smith's "self" had ever been just this collection of habits, abilities, feelings, sensations, and performances, there is no *scientific* reason to believe that this "self" would survive the transplantation intact. And, for the very same reasons, we should not expect that Jones will have Smith's "self" or Jones's. By the time the relocated brain and its new quarters become accustomed to one another, some new "self" will have arisen and neither Smith's nor Jones's will be anywhere to be found. I do not want to press this analysis too hard, but it is of sufficient merit to claim at least parity with the more common and now not at all obvious alternative. If my own expectations were confirmed scientifically, therefore, we would not be on firm ground in claiming that every or any psychological state or event can be no more than a process in the brain. We might be inclined to believe that at least Smith's memories will be relocated in the new body, but even this relatively modest proposal faces hardships. Smith and Jones may, of course, have the same memories quite apart from swapping brains. The central question is whether Smith's memories—*as Smith's*—are now (somehow) "in" Jones's body. For this to be the case, there would have to be the continuing existence of that "self" who was Smith (when in Smith's body) but it is just this continuity that the transplantation disrupts. The alternative I have been defending would result in alarming doubts as to whose memories are now recalled with this brain in a different body.

The Identity Thesis, which I have discussed in other places,[22] runs into similar technical problems in addition to very serious conceptual ones. To claim, as J. J. C. Smart has claimed, that "Sensations are brain processes"[23] is to trivialize both sensations and brain processes. Sensations are the complex consequence of environmental impingements on sensory organs and the processing of neural signals arising from these organs. The brain, receiving these signals, is also receiving signals from the balance of the body, and sending signals to the body—including the sensory mechanisms as well—in virtually continuous and closed-loop fashion. The term "brain process" is actually more akin to "digestion" or "metabolism" than to any unitary occurrence with definable location and bounded onset and offset times. What is event-like in the brain is so by virtue of our methods of investigation, which tend to take still photographs and not motion pictures.

There are, of course, occurrences in the brain that are phase-locked to stimuli or with which certain rudimentary motor events are phase-locked. But even in these instances, both the brain and the peripheral event are governed in their activity by the entire history of the organism; by past sensations, actions, agings and performances. Accordingly, sensations are not merely brain processes even in the scientific sense, and therefore cannot be merely brain processes in any sense.

Defenders of the Identity Thesis might enlarge their hypothesis to include what we already know about the physiology of sensation. They might say that, "Sensations are physiological processes," and avoid the Wittgensteinian problem of reference by declaring that, if "sensations" refers to anything, it refers to physiological processes in the body of the percipient. Stated this way, the thesis claims that sensations (or, by extension, all mental events) are not caused by physiological processes but just *are* these processes; i.e., physiological processes and mental events are *identical*.

How this proposed identity is to be taken is not entirely clear, however. It surely is not a formal identity, for if it were then *necessarily* every mental event would be a brain process. This cannot be so, for if it were then any denial of the proposition would involve a logical contradiction. Nor can the identity come about by way of a veiled tautology such that all mental events are physiological processes in just the way that all unmarried men are bachelors. Surely "mental events" doesn't *mean* physiological processes, and we can say many true things about mental events that cannot be said about physiological processes; e.g., I experience my mental events directly, whereas I know about my physiological processes only by description.

Might the relationship be, as Smart has wondered, of the Morning Star–Evening Star variety, the so-called Phosphorus-Hesperus problem? Is it the case that what is said of Phosphorus can be said of Hesperus, *salva veritate*, because, "Phosphorus is Hesperus" is tautologously true? This matter enjoys a veritable tradition in Philosophy and, as of now, our answers to such questions have to be of the "that depends" variety. The tradition, which has Medieval roots, surfaces in modern times in the form of this pair of observations:

1. The Morning Star *is* the Evening Star but,
2. The claim in (1) is informative in a way that neither "The Morning Star is the Morning Star" nor "The Evening Star is the Evening Star" is.

Thus, if (1) is non-trivially true—in that it expresses a discovered fact of nature—then it is not a tautology. Yet, "Morning Star" and "Evening Star" refer to the same entity.

Imagine a tribe in which two distinct forms of defective color vision were present; a form of dichromatism whose sufferers were insensitive to red and another form whose sufferers were insensitive to green. A stranger comes to the village. He has red hair and green eyes. Half the tribe comes to know him as "Red" but can recognize him only in the light of day. The other half comes to know him as "Green" but, because of an additional visual defect, can only recognize him after the sun goes down. Later, through improved diet and corrective lenses, every member of the tribe gains normal vision and discovers that "Red" is "Green." The stranger's name is actually Smith.

1. Smith is Smith (Law of Identities)
2. Everything true of Smith is true of Smith. (Law of Identities)
3. "Red" and "Green" are conventional names given to Smith. (fact)
4. Everything physically true of Smith is true of "Red" and "Green." (Law of Identities)
5. There is someone who does not know (1)–(4) under condition C.

What should be clear from this is that nothing about *Smith* is affected by (5), and that condition C is a description not of Smith but of an observation. From the logical rule according to which everything is identical to itself, it does not follow that every *observation* of a thing is identical to every other *observation* of it. Thus, Hesperus is Phosphorous analytically, though no given observation of Hesperus is necessarily an observation of Phosphorus for no two observations are ever *necessarily* identical. I leave this unavoidable digression by emphasizing that, whatever the identity of *mental events* and *physiological processes*, it is not of the Phosphorus-Hesperus variety, for it is not analytic. "Hesperus is Hesperus" is not an observation.

We are left, therefore, only with the possibility that mental events are *contingently identical* with physiological processes, the possibility recommended by Smart himself.[24] The celebrated example of contingent identity has a person using the telephone. We shall call him Smith. Jones, who knows Smith, says to Brown, "Smith is on the telephone." White, who does not know Smith, says to Black, "Someone is on the telephone." As it happens, "Someone" and "Smith" refer to the same person and thus, "Someone" and "Smith" are said to be *contingent identities*. But this will not work. It is the case, of course, that of all the persons who might have been using the telephone Smith (contingently) is the one who is actually using it. But it would be bizarre to assert that, of all the persons Smith might be, he is (contingently) the one he is! The Smith–Someone pairing is a formal identity whereas "being on the telephone" is an activity. No activity is logically necessary. Smith just happens to be on the phone, but he does not just happen to be himself.

Not only is there something peculiar about the notion of Smith being "contingently" identical to someone but, as Saul Kripke[25] and others have argued, the very concept of a contingent identity is oxymoronic or at least ambiguous. As I have noted elsewhere[26] the identity thesis has the additional burden of being inconsequential in that, were it true, *nothing would change!* That is, on the assumption that every mental event is unfailingly a brain-event or process, the recorded, current, and future mental events of the human race remain utterly unaffected by the fact. Hopes, fears, desires, motives, memories, concepts, plans, curiosities, creations, and dilemmas are exactly what they are—even as many persons proceed in their "mental" lives without having a hint that all of these events just *are* processes occurring in their craniums. We don't even have the promise of scientific confirmation, for as Smart himself observed there is no possible experiment that would permit us to choose between this thesis and such alternatives as psychophysical parallelism and epiphenomenalism.[27] In light of this, the thesis itself is not to be regarded as a scientific thesis since the latter species is reserved for propositions that are at least in principle decided by empirical findings.

Actually, the case against neurophysiological theories of mental life is somewhat stronger than might appear at first blush, even in this era of technical and scientific progress in the neural sciences. There are, of course, the well-known correlations between neuropathology and psychological deficits, not to mention the veritable handbook of scientific studies linking psychological states to events occurring or induced in brain tissue. But a neurophysiological *theory* of mental life must go beyond such observed correlations and attempt to provide the explanation for them. Theories, as I have noted, are not descriptive or predictive alone, but explanatory. The most plausible theory in the present context is one that would assign *causal* properties to the brain and would therefore be a version of epiphenomenalism. This seems to be the most plausible for, unlike the identity thesis or eliminative materialism, epiphenomenalism at least grants the mind and mental life existential status, even if a depreciated and utterly dependent one.

But if versions of epiphenomenalism are plausible in their ontologies, they are less so as causal explanations. Once mental events are granted, we still must choose a set of attributes by which any candidate-event may be assigned to the category of "mental," and one of these attributes must be nonphysical. Somewhere along the line the epiphenomenalist must be willing to have a "ghost in the machine" (*pace* Ryle) that is distinguishable from any of the machine's moving (massive) parts; and if not a ghost, at least ghost-like phenomena so-called because they cannot be completely or even partly described in the language of Physics. Somewhere along the line, for example, the epiphenomenalist must be willing to posit a *self* in which various sensations and feelings inhere; a *self* that has the necessary possessory rights with respect to ideas, plans, intentions, etc. (since every idea is *someone's*).

We could of course attempt to avoid all possible contamination by spiritism and say only that every idea (or pain or feeling) is some *brain's* idea (or pain or feeling) but success at this sort of ploy must be illusory. We do not produce a causal theory of a physicalistic sort by assigning to the brain all of the mental states and attributes customarily assigned to persons. This is an illicit step, not a reductive one. If the task is to provide a causal theory of the *experience* of pain or of the *having* of an idea, nothing is gained by giving the experience or the possession to the brain, for now we have to explain how a brain experiences pain or has an idea. Note, then, that the dilemma remains as long as we retain nonphysical events or attributes and is not in any way resolved by moving these events or attributes from one place to another.

There is no epoch so brief as to record a *permanent* state within any cell of the body, including the brain. Cellular life is continuous and dynamic. Nonetheless, there are psychological states or mental properties that may remain stable for fractions of a lifetime. The very continuity of one's *self* is illustrative of permanence in the face of biological change. Thus, a neurophysiological *causal* theory of mental life suffers the problem of *phase* in that the relevant time-constants in the two domains are often and totally incompatible. Nor is this problem defeated by appeals to the notion of recurring states that are the "same," for the attribute of *sameness* can only be assigned from a position external to the system. From whose (what) perspective is neural state-A the *same* as neural state-B? Then, too, there is the problem of localization. Every process in the brain can be located within a three-dimensional coordinate system, though it would be droll to say the same of a desire or a judgment or a promise. The point here is not that we cannot say with some propriety that Smith makes promises *only* when Smith's brain is in state-X, but that statements of this type cannot be shown to be part of some larger causal script. Smith also makes promises (a) only when prepared to do so; (b) only when called upon to do so; (c) only when awake; (d) only to members of his own family; (e) only during the course of his life; (f) only in writing.

The greatest problem by far, however, is the striking and qualitative mismatch between anything physical and anything mental. When Berkeley argued that an idea can be like nothing but another idea he was defending an immaterialism that need not be invoked here, but he was also noting the *sui generis* status of mental constructs. An idea is just not like an object or any part thereof. We can conceive of events in the brain causally determining other physical events, including all the movements by the body, the secretions of the glands, and so forth. But from the ionic movements that constitute the neural impulse we cannot construct a promise or a pain. How, then, can we construct a promise or a pain from ionic movements in two such neurons, or twenty-two or twenty-two million? I do not here fall back on those ancient and medieval notions according to which X cannot be the cause of Y unless X and Y have something in common, though these are notions not to be dismissed lightly. After all, neural and mental events are cotemporaneous, so they do have at least something in common. Rather, I am noting a distinction that is entirely obvious to the Plain Man and that will not be removed

by a wave of the hand. It is the distinction between *any* introspectively authenticated event and *any* ostensively definable entity, including a brain-process.

The usual counter to this argument from incommensurability is one or another form of *emergentism*, but this turns out
to be a begging and not an answering of the question. It is simply
contingently true that no observable property of a network of neural
units is different in kind from properties observed in single units.
Depending on the level of analysis, these properties are exhausted by the processes of excitation, inhibition, fatigue, and
structural change. The typical emergentist exemplum—that H_2O
has properties not found either in H_2 or O_2—is beside the point
in at least two ways. First of all, all of the properties of H_2O
chemically discernible are *physical* properties and therefore the example is not an example of the emergence of a new class of properties. It is true that H_2O has certain *phenomenal* properties (such
as wetness) not shared by the molecules of the constituent gasses,
but it is just these phenomenal properties we're trying to explain.
Nothing about the *chemistry* of oxygen or hydrogen or water explains *any* experience we have when we are in contact with O_2, H_2
or H_2O. Secondly, it is not clear that something has "emerged"
out of the combination of the gasses. Surely any exhaustive and
exclusively physical description of O_2 will include the fact that,
when united in the proper combination with H_2, it will (for example) dissolve salts and retain heat. Nor is there any physical
mystery about how H_2O comes to be a solvent in a way that neither H_2 nor O_2 is. But a statement of the sort,

> "Given enough H_2 and O_2, properly combined, and x grams of NaCl
> will be dissolved"

is radically different from a statement of the sort,

> "Given enough H_2 and O_2, properly combined, and the commit-
> ment to change beneficiaries in the will shall be causally brought
> about."

The radical difference is not the result of H_2O having no central
function in neural transmission or synaptic physiology, but in

person and his pains fall within a common boundary. We can establish the boundary of the person without his help—even if he is dead—but we cannot locate his pains this way.

The criterion of publicity referred to earlier is scientifically vital, but we must be cautious in the implications we draw having imposed it. Smith sees White in a crowd and announces, "There's White." Jones, looking from a different angle, replies, "Yes, it's White." We can say they both see the same person, but not that they both have the same perception. Smith sits before a split screen, one half of which contains a colored light which he must match in the other half by adjusting dials controlling the amount of red, blue, and green (plus intensity) appearing in the test-field. Smith manipulates the dials and announces, "The two fields are perfectly matched." Jones performs the task, but Jones suffers from a form of dichromatism and is utterly insensitive to red. Thus, in achieving a match, he takes no account of the red in the standard field. After adjusting the dials he announces, "The two fields are perfectly matched." We now inspect the two sets of dial settings and discover that Smith added x units of red but Jones added none. What shall we say? Did they have different experiences? Yes and no. Both of them (truthfully) reported that the two fields were perfectly matched, so both of them had the experience of a perfect match, so both of them had the same experience. But one of them can't see red and the other can, so they obviously did not see the same stimulus properties. But there is no way to tell what it means to "experience" red except by consulting our own experiences (our own "beetles") or, in a scientific context, by measuring either the range of wavelengths over which cooperative observers continue to apply the name "red" or the amount of "red"-correlated wavelengths observers add in achieving a color match. If we say to Jones, "You didn't use any red in your match," it is not clear what he can make of the statement, since we're referring to a "beetle" he has never seen. Actually, the light Smith saw was not "red"; it was a light whose maximum transmission was in the range of 720–740 nanometers. But Smith does not *see* wavelengths, he *sees* colors. Thus, it would be uninforming to say that Jones did not *see* 740 nanometers, for no one sees such items. What

Smith and Jones saw, in a manner of speaking, was what was there for each of them. But the only basis upon which we can *finally* regard their experiences as different is self-referential. We know what red looks like and *we* know that the two fields will not be matched unless red is added to one of them. Jones's vision is *defective*, then, only on the assumption that his reports are to be trusted and then compared with our own. It is only by accepting his claim that the match is perfect that we have any justification for assuming that he lacks red-sensitivity.

Here, then, we have the now celebrated *incorrigibility* attribute that attaches to all cooperative reports of experience.[30] What Smith or Jones or anyone else says about an experience— a pain, a color, a sentiment—cannot be corrected from the outside. Such reports are *incorrigible* in that only the percipient has the last word on what that percipient is experiencing. If Smith says, "I see it as red," we can say the experience is illusory or odd or not grounded in fact or the result of pathology, but we cannot say, "No you don't" and make it stick. Again, the so-called private language problem is a philosophical digression. What is private about Smith's experience is the epistemic proprietorship he has over it, not the language he uses to describe it. But neither he nor anyone else enjoys the same privileged position regarding *any* statement made about *any* brain process, including the reporter's own. One may always be provably wrong in identifying or describing a physiological event; one is never *provably* wrong in identifying or describing a (private) sensation.

It is this incorrigibility that arises from and at the same time does much to establish the incommensurability obtaining between physical and mental phenomena. An idea is *like* only another idea, a pain *like* only another pain. But we go beyond Berkeley here in recognizing that the likeness is not merely phenomenal but epistemological. There is no theoretical limit to the level of detail that might be attained in our knowledge and description of neural processes until we reach the subatomic level. The problem of "reduction," therefore, is not technical as such but conceptual. To what might the reporter's *incorrigibility* claims be reduced? The very question underscores the incommensurability of physical and mental events. The so-called "central state materialist"[31] who would "reduce" the experience of pain to some (in principle) describable state of the nervous system is no better off in dealing with incorrigibility. What "state" of the nervous system confers on the percipient's reports of pain the incorrigibility they enjoy, but withholds it from the percipient's report that it is raining? When Smith says it is raining he is making a factual claim regarding the experiences others would have were they looking at what Smith is looking at. What is different about Smith's statement that he is in pain is not that it is any less factual but that *only he* can, as it were, look at "it." This is true of no "central state," for any such state can in principle be looked at by anyone competent to investigate the central nervous system.

There is, alas, more than one respect in which the various "solutions" to the Mind/Body problem fail as reductive accounts. With both epiphenomenalism and the Identity thesis, the psychological side of the equation remains as populous as it is in the hands of the mentalist, so there is no reduction at all. With Eliminative or Central State materialism there is, finally, no *causal* explanation forthcoming, for neither can overcome the problem of incommensurability. And where there is no causal explanation there is no reduction, for all causal explanations of a scientific nature are reductive. Mimimally, a causal explanation is one that identifies the (minimum) conditions unfailingly sufficient to bring about an event—the *conditio sine qua non*. But this is achieved scientifically only through bridging laws which have in common the rejection of a once alleged incommensurability between the independent and the dependent variables. Thus, the causal explanation of lightning becomes possible once we know that the movement of charged particles can simulate the effect; i.e., that there is no fundamental incommensurability between electrical phenomena and those traditionally referred to as "lightning." Eliminative materialism is not reductive: it does not reduce the number of mental entities; it denies that there are any. But the success available to defenders of this thesis can be secured only after it is shown that there is no reliable "mental" entity or attribute for which a commensurable neural entity or attribute is lacking. Again, what might the neural equivalent of *incorrigibility* be? And what might the neural equivalent of *privacy* be?

Artificial Intelligence and Computer Simulations

Having addressed elsewhere[32] the limitations of computer science in the matter of modeling psychological processes, I will only offer some general considerations in this section. Perhaps the most general has to do with the illicit nature of the alleged "reductions" achieved by this approach. As discussed in the two preceding sections, even the illicit reductions are not really reductive, but it is their illicit nature that is of concern here. I should say first, however, that in discussing artificial intelligence (AI) and computer simulations, I shall disregard the important practical and technical accomplishments earned in these fields, and confine my remarks only to those undertakings designed to explain or reductively account for human psychological processes, either perceptual or cognitive. (We can agree that the tape recorder is a wonderful device without regarding it as a contribution to our knowledge of human memory!)

There are several superficial resemblances shared by a modern computer facility and the sorts of things done by human beings as perceivers, cognizers, memorizers, and problem-solvers. The resemblances are scarcely accidental, since the machinery was designed to mimic these very processes. The question that arises, in light of the successful mimicry, is whether the human functions are best understood (explained) as a species of the types of functions incorporated into these devices.

In a computer facility there is first a technique for getting data into the system; for having an *input format* compatible with the processor-mechanisms which are usually of the "microchip" variety, and with the "machine-language" in which various programs are written. In most systems, inputs can be typed or "keyed" directly. The consequence of the operator's typing is to activate specific microcircuits that are hard-wired to treat the input in specific ways. (There may also be a "learning" feature such that the microcircuits actually undergo changes as a function of previous inputs but, as we shall see, this is less relevant to the central issue than it might appear to be.) The parallel with human perceptual functions is not hard to see. The external world impinges on sense organs which transduce the input into a format (electrical) compatible with the "machine language" of the nervous system.

Within the central processor (the "brain") of the system, the various electrical events are governed by a specific program; or, better, the various electrical events are designed to *realize* a specific program which may call for arithmetic operations or chess moves or the activation of an associated speech-synthesizer. From the user's perspective, the electrical events are invisible and useless. What is needed is an appropriate *output format* that is provided in the user's language; e.g., printed numbers, printed words, intelligible speech, etc. Thus, between the central processor and the readout device, there must be some sort of dictionary or *algorithm* by which to translate each term in the processor's language into a term in the user's language. What is occurring in the processor, of course, is the movement of electrical pulses through pathways organized as printed circuits. The trick is to have these pulses finally activate a readout device whose output is in the user's language.

Again, at first blush, this seems to be just what the human "processor" is designed to do. The external world impinges on the sense organs, by transduction these stimuli are coded into electrical pulses, which move along the complex anatomical paths (the circuitry) of the nervous system, arrive at various locations within the brain (the central processor), and are organized according to a "program," partly genetic (pre-wired) and partly learned. In turn, the brain's outputs are all electrical and must activate a readout mechanism so that the percipient (the "user") gets not the electrical pulses but, for example, a tree bending in the wind on a sunny day in November.

If this is to be achieved, then we too need some sort

of *algorithm* by which the pulse-coded outputs of the brain are translated into the user's language. But for such a translation to occur, it is necessary that the system possess at least two languages, for the process of translation entails at least two languages. In the present case, the languages would have to be (a) the electrical one that is the machine language of the brain and (b) a phenomenal or experiential one whose elements include such entries as "tree," "sunny," "bending." However, with human beings (or higher animals of any stripe), there is only one way into the brain, and that is via the sense organs. Thus, the only language we can ever get *to the brain* is the machine language itself; viz., pulse-coded electrical signals. There is no way of getting "tree" or "sunny" or "bending" to the brain, and so there is no way of constructing an algorithm from within that could possibly translate electrical pulses into anything but electrical pulses. Recall that with computers *we* write the programs and *we* provide the translation algorithms. A computer system, equipped with sensors and exposed to the crisp air of November may well yield, THERE IS A TREE BENDING IN THE WIND . . . IT IS A SUNNY DAY . . . IT IS NOVEMBER. But it does so only because percipients who have experienced trees bending in the wind on sunny November days have seen fit to program a device to provide such outputs when certain information is read into it. With the brain, however, the rule is *pulses in* and *pulses out* with narry a tree to be found!

Translation entails not merely multiple languages but a knowledge of same. For the brain, via some "translational" algorithm, to achieve successful translations, the brain would have to know (somehow) both its own machine language and the language into which its own is to be translated. On the (radically) materialistic thesis according to which we are only our brains, this amounts to saying that brains must know both brain-terms and phenomenal terms. If nothing else, however, this would mean that there could not possibly be a scientific question regarding the "language of the brain," for we (brains) surely know this language or could not translate it into any other. As it happens, however, thousands of scientists over the past two centuries have labored diligently to unearth just this "language of the brain," and only with mixed and incomplete success. Clearly, either the brain as brain has no language—and thus can't do any of these things—or *dualism* is necessarily true, or both.

What creates the impression that AI and computer simulations are relevant to reductionism is the failure to appreciate the extent to which the psychological side of the equation remains entirely *outside* such simulations. Within the devices there are only moving parts; no words, thoughts, hopes, feelings, judgments, confusions, expectations. The simulation has no "language"—machine or otherwise—but only a design that permits *us* to use it for certain linguistic transactions. When we speak on the telephone, the telephone isn't saying anything. Interestingly, the brain itself is finally but a congeries of moving parts which can no more have a language than a sense of humor. That we need such moving parts for us to have a language is contingently the case during this, our sublunary life, but this requirement is not unlike needing an amplifier if we would be heard. To think otherwise is to traffic in a kind of superstition and to confer on mere *things* all sorts of dark powers and magical potentialities. Dualism may lack economy and neatness, but it is by far less *spooky* than the now popular alternative.

Summary

The three major programs of reductionistic psychology are the behavioristic, the neurological, and the computational. All are finally materialistic in that all seek to "neurologize" mental entities and anchor them to purely physical processes. Each deals with the embarrassment of *private* mental events in a different but an equally unsuccessful way; either by assuming there is a problem where there is none (e.g., the "private-language" pseudoproblem); or by assuming there is no problem when indeed there is (the materialist's inability to deal with psychophysical incommensurability and with the incorrigibility of first-person accounts of mental events); or by re-creating the problem in a merely distracting setting (e.g., computer "simulations").

Mentalism, at least in its non-gaudy forms, survives all of these programs and alerts psychologists to the requirement that mental life must be dealt with in its own terms. The primary data of Psychology remain introspective, no matter how these data are later coded or transformed for purposes of analysis. The fundamental issues in Psychology are the gift of these data and cannot be traded in for more tractable issues in biology, computer science, or animal behavior.

CHAPTER FOUR

Explanations

The principal aim of psychological discourse, research, and theory is of course to produce explanations. At the philosophical or metapsychological level, it is necessary to establish the criteria of explanation so that the productions of the discipline can be tested against more or less settled standards of explanatory rigor, validity, and completeness.

We owe to Carl Hempel the revival and refinement of a model of scientific explanation that is at least implicit in the works of many older commentators from Aristotle on.[1] The model—called *nomological-deductive* or "covering law"—is one that regards events as scientifically explained when they are shown to be instances of a universal law not violated by any known fact or observation. Thus, all other relevant conditions being equal, we have *explained* the free-fall behavior of an object by invoking a (Newtonian) gravitational law that covers all such events. The scientific answer to the question of why such objects fall is nothing more than and nothing different from a statement of the law itself. Hempel himself has argued that the model is fully applicable to the social sciences[2] but many commentators have offered a variety of criticisms against this view, and others have rejected the model even when applied to the physical sciences.[3] It will be useful to set up several of the more compelling arguments for and against the nomological-deductive model as a brief introduction to the problem of explanation in general and in the "human sciences" in particular.

For the Nomological-Deductive Model

As a model of scientific explanation, the "covering law" approach is largely indifferent to nuances of method and subject-matter, and is therefore open to the wide range of scientific endeavors. It leaves as much room for a possibly scientific History or Psychology or Economics as for such traditional sciences as Physics and Chemistry. What confers scientific status on an enterprise is the logic of its explanatory statements; as long as these are confined to empirical events and are grounded in true universal laws, they are *scientific* whatever their subject-matter or particular methods may be.

As indicative of what the established sciences have been historically, the covering-law model has the added advantage of being compatible with the classical achievements in Physics, Chemistry, and Biology. The gravitational laws of Newton, the gas laws of Boyle and Charles, the astronomical laws of Kepler and the mechanical laws of Galileo are illustrative. What we generally regard to be the very best scientific explanations, coming from the most developed branches of scientific knowledge, are those grounded in universal laws of exceptionless reliability. We also expect—as the covering-law model requires—a symmetry to obtain between explanation and prediction such that the statements in the science that are explanatory with respect to what has occurred are the same statements offered as accounts of what will occur. Putting this another way, and referring back to topics discussed in chapter 2, we expect scientific statements to be not only predictive but predictive in contrary-to-fact conditional contexts. Given the universal law, we can say not merely what *will* happen, but what *would* happen *were* such and such conditions to obtain. A scientific explanation is not therefore simply an empirical generalization or a summary of data at hand.

Against the Nomological-Deductive Model

Criticisms have been arrayed against the model from a variety of perspectives, not all of them compatible with the rest, though neither singly nor collectively have they constituted an alternative *model*. They fall into distinguishable if occasionally overlapping classes.[4]

1. *Exclusivity*: In light of the criteria demanded by the model, it has been argued that bona fide scientific work is excluded. Note, for example, that evolutionary theory does not possess universal laws and does not display symmetry between explanation and prediction. The basis upon which variations among species are explained does not provide us with a means by which to anticipate what the long-term future of the animal kingdom will yield. Even the alleged universal law of "natural selection" is an after-the-fact postulate. Only from the *fact* that a species has survived can we say that its nuances are the gift of "selection." The "law," then, may be said to be instantiated by a given species but is never predictive of one. Accordingly, explanations grounded in evolutionary concepts are not scientific (or not yet scientific), and this seems to be at variance with our intuitive understanding. It is, the critics say, just counterintuitive to declare that the theory of evolution is not a scientific theory.

Recall that there is no universal law to be found in Economics, Sociology, Psychology, Anthropology, or even in many branches of Biology and Chemistry. Are all of these to be excluded from the province of science? Then, too, at the subatomic level of observation we discover that troublesome *uncertainty* discussed in chapter 2; a veritable *principle of uncertainty* which legislates against the very nomic necessity upon which the covering-law model would seem to depend. Is the entire field of particle-Physics to be excluded from the domain in which scientific explanations are fashioned?

2. *The Fallacy of Omniscience*: The covering-law model requires that the universal laws invoked to explain phenomena be true, for the very compelling reason that a false law explains nothing! But how do we know that a law is true? Might not the future disconfirm even our most settled laws, and must we then reach the counterintuitive conclusion that our earlier explanations were not only wrong but *unscientific*? The inescapable burden of human fallibility imposes limitations on our grasp of truth. We can *never* say that a nontautologous statement is *true come what may*, and so we can never say that a law of science is *true come what may*. To accept the nomological-deductive model is, then, to reject the very possibility of science.

3. *Ideographic vs. Nomothetic Explanation*:[5] Human beings, and for that matter all advanced species, are biogenetically unique and thus develop in a manner that expresses the unique interaction between a given member of the species and the complex nurturing environments in which it has been placed. The human personality is formed and sustained not only by complex and elusive variables, but also by those that differ from one person to the next. Any explanation of *psychological* attributes must be tailor-made to fit the unduplicated aspects of the life of the given individual. To be able to say why Smith does this or that or will do this or that requires that we know about Smith, and not simply about the species of which Smith is a member. There are, of course, certain processes (e.g., sensory, digestive, reflexive) common to all normal members of the species and *nomothetic* explanation is possible with respect to these. This is not the case, however, with respect to any complex psychological process, such as volition, motivation, emotion, creativity, conviction, and the like.

4. *Irreducibly Social Phenomena*: When it comes to significant human endeavors, the covering-law model is simply inapplicable, for what gives such endeavors their identifying character is the mixture of utterly individualistic motives, reasons, strategies, and objectives. Social and historical phenomena are not just

so many balls rolling down so many inclined planes.[6] One cannot even describe such phenomena without including irreducibly psychological (emotive, motivational, rational) terms, and one would not find intelligible any explanation of them devoid of the same terms.

5. *The Sociology of Science*: What the covering-law model ignores, and what gives it its artificial nature, is the fact that science is done by actual persons whose undertakings occur within definable historical and social and personal contexts. These psychosocial conditions cannot be removed from science, and a given scientific endeavor can never be totally divorced from them.[7] Like shoes and ships, a society *makes* science and makes it for social purposes. Every now and then and unpredictably there is a tumultuous or revolutionary breakthrough in what is typically the normal life of science. But on the whole the scientific endeavor is one guided by well worn "paradigms" of a conservative nature expressive of the social history and the social context within which the science was forged and by which its fate is determined.

These five classes of criticism are not exhaustive, but they cover most of the grounds on which rejections of the model have been based. They are formidable but not fatal criticisms and we should review at least in general terms how the model might be defended against them.

Replies to #1: As a model of scientific explanation, the nomological-deductive criteria are intended to be exclusive, but not in the static or eternal sense. Thus, a given explanation (e.g., evolutionary theory) may fail to qualify as a scientific explanation for reasons that may be overcome by future research, observations, and conceptualizations. Presumably, the molar facts of evolution express more fundamental events occurring at the level of molecular biology. Bridging laws are conceivable by which we can move from the molecular biology of the gene to the phenotypic characters conferring adaptive potential on the species. With even further progress, it may be possible to specify relationships between molecular phenomena and any given ecological circumstance, thereby rendering evolutionary explanations symmetrical with predictions of imminent species variations. Lacking these bridges and lacking embracing covering laws, fields such as Evolutionary Biology, Economics, Psychology, and the rest cannot now offer scientific explanations but (*via* reliable empirical laws) can provide "explanation-sketches"[8] that hold out the promise of an ultimate nomological-deductive framework. Exclusion, therefore, may be only temporary. In any case, the exclusionary principles constitute the definable goal toward which aspiring sciences should aim.

Replies to #2: It goes without saying that we may always be wrong in our statements about nature, including our nomic statements. However, from the fact of fallibility we are not to derive permission for anarchy! We can all agree that what is provably false is never an explanation. Thus, scientific explanations, if framed in the language of laws, must be erected on true laws. That the future may embarrass our confidence is a possibility that must be faced with eagerness, not anxiety; and surely not dubiety. Still, during any specific interval of scientific activity, we must have some standard of truth to which we submit our laws; and when the best tests are passed, we have no alternative but to accept the laws as true. Typically, advances in science are not at the total expense of an earlier nomological-deductive system, but require a modification of it. We do not say in the wake of Relativity Theory that Newton was wrong, but that the Newtonian formulations are true within boundary-conditions once thought to be limitless. There is a space-time coordinate system within which Newtonian explanations continue to be instantiated and within which Newtonian predictions are faultlessly confirmed *wherever* the observations are made within that system. Newton did not know that at super-velocities mass undergoes change, but this fact has no bearing— practical or theoretical—on the explanations and predictions offered of the behavior of objects moving at velocities significantly less than the speed of light.

Replies to #3 and #4: There is nothing in the nomological-deductive model that requires *physical* causation of events, only *lawful* causation. If the "law" of supply and demand were universally true, the discipline of Economics would possess scientific explanations whether or not such a law was ultimately grounded in more basic laws of Physics. The model is ontologically neutral as to the kinds of basic "stuff" actually existing in the universe, leaving as much room in principle for mental or motivational entities as for electrical or atomic ones. The critic who insists that persons are unique and are uniquely affected by their environments must base this claim on observations. If the claim is true, the observations are reliable. And if the observations are reliable, they can be subsumed under a (provisional) statistical law which, itself, may well be grounded in a more fundamental universal law. Idiosyncrasy alone does not disqualify an event or item (or person) from scientific study or scientific explanation. If, however, there is a defensible and principled argument according to which *nothing* of a lawful nature can be said about the behavior or psychology of persons, then it follows that no scientific explanation is possible. It just follows that the disciplines accepting proprietorship of such phenomena cannot be scientific and should attempt to develop standards of explanation independently of those applicable to science.

Replies to #5: Whether or not the Kuhnian "paradigms" amount to any more than what Popper has called "the myth of framework,"[9] they are scarcely sufficient to sustain an essentially sociological view of science. Science is done by human beings, even for human beings, but this would seem to have no more bearing on the essential character of science than it does on the essential character of Plane Geometry. We can accept that scientists approach their work with various motives and under the influence of various historical (biographical) and social forces without granting that the work itself must carry these stamps or ever has carried them. What social fact or biographical detail of the life of Archimedes must be taken into account as we attempt to determine the *scientific* standing of his laws of buoancy? The factors that impel persons toward or away from rationality are distinct from the logical criteria that are invoked to determine whether an argument is sound, coherent, or self-refuting. Let us say that under the celebrated influence of Newton's Physics, John Locke was inclined to develop a mental science of a corpuscular nature in which associative principles were to do the work of gravity. This claim, if true, would help us understand why, of all the models of the mind that Locke might have chosen, he favored one that was compatible with Newton's model of the universe. But the claim, true or false, is utterly beside the point of whether or not Locke's theory of ideation is correct. It is simply a species of the *ad hominem* fallacy to conflate assessments of a scientific thesis with assessments of the "psychology" of the person who advances it. Scientific theories are, to be sure, perspectival and can be replaced by massive shifts in perspective. This possibility is at the root of the Duhem-Quine thesis which allows any theory to be rendered conformable to the facts if we are willing to make radical enough adjustments to the system as a whole.[10] But when all of this is completed, we are still obliged to submit our adjustments and our radically altered perspective to tests of internal coherence and external correspondence with the facts themselves. The potential for "pluralism" resides not in the tests or the standards of truth but in the variety of ways such tests and standards might be satisfied. The laws of motion can be summarized either through a differential calculus applied to the unfolding phenomena themselves or an integral calculus that embraces the completed behavior of the system. Whichever the chosen method, the laws of motion must be equally and perfectly described. Whim may explain the choice of mathematical approaches but not the standard either approach must satisfy. In a word, there is a sociology of scientists, but not of science *qua* science. For the latter, we have only a logical, not a sociological framework.

What Makes an Explanation "Good"?

This is not the place to decide for or against the nomological-deductive model. The criticisms against it are not frivolous and the replies to them are neither entirely successful nor unsuccessful. What the model captures is the aesthetic appeal held forth by a set of explanations marking out the theoretical domain of classical Physics. Perhaps it is only within that domain that such explanations ever could have been minted. But the aesthetic dimension is not to be depreciated, even if it does imply subjectivity and the vagaries of fashion. The aesthetic dimension is not engaged, we should recall, until the explanations have recommended themselves on all of the other and objective bases: completeness, predictive efficiency, accuracy, confirmation, symmetry. Only when two competing explanations are equally *good* do we ask which is more "elegant" (as mathematicians use the term) or more parsimonious or more coherent.

As suggested in chapter 1, in connection with Dante's apparition, it is not the public record of perceptions that stands as the court of final recourse in matters of explanation. Explanations may be disconfirmed by facts, but not finally sanctioned by them. Allegedly true accounts of the world must correspond to the observable events in the world but they must do more. They must provide a *coherent* account and not merely a catalogue of these events. Explanation is more than taxonomy, more than description. It has a certain narrative property that imposes an inevitability on the occurrences it reports. In classical Physics this inevitability is guaranteed by the *nomic necessity* of scientific laws (chapter 2), but the inevitability it seems must be found elsewhere when the phenomena of human actions are the subject of study. Before testing this claim we should examine just what we are looking for in any explanation and why we want one in the first place.

Some perceived regularities in nature are so abundant and invariant that the events are obviously answerable to a law of nature. If only because of the predictive power such laws confer, we have strong pragmatic reasons for looking for them. Where the regularities are less consistent but at least suggestive, science has shown that the careful and proper partitioning of the sources of variation will often disclose an invariant relationship. The record to date strongly supports the belief that, with respect to purely physical happenings at the molar level of observation, there is an inviolable law of nature at work. Once discovered, the law obviates the need for further observation, since we now know how the variables will behave within those boundaries set by the

law itself. Technical advances may permit an expansion of the observation space and tests to determine the fuller range over which
the law has its dispository powers. New laws may have to be framed
to accommodate violations occurring in contexts not initially envisaged. This, in capsule form, has been the progress of science
since at least the seventeenth century. It is the story of science.

But it is a story that we do not and perhaps cannot
tell from the beginning. We have explained the free-fall behavior
of an object by invoking the law according to which objects att-
ract each other with a force proportional to the product of their
masses and inversely proportional to the squared distance between them. But our story does not explain *why* these forces are
as they are or *why* they are diminished in proportion to the *squared*
distance. Scientific explanations are *ultimate* not in the sense of
being exhaustive but in the sense of establishing where on the
continuum of time human knowledge must begin its accounts. With
respect to the phenomena embraced by them, scientific explanations are "good" chiefly because they can be no better.

To move to an earlier point on the continuum we must
abandon the reassurances of knowledge *per se* and accept the mixed
bounty of what is finally a metaphysical and not a scientific understanding. At this point the price we pay for a consistent and
coherent "world view" is any number of antinomies, conundrums,
paradoxes, and exceptions. Again, the "ultimate" nature of scientific explanations is less a matter of the success of science than
of the failure of alternatives. At present, science will sustain to
varying degrees both a "big bang" and a "continuous creation"
account of the very existence of the universe, the more recent formulations tending to support the former. The scientific explanation is at last a summary of those conditions that would be causally
sufficient to account for the observable data. To ask whether, for
example, an explanation grounded in theology is "better" is actually to seek a comparison of incommensurables. Where the theological account assumes the actions of an intelligent being, the
resulting explanation is entirely indifferent to considerations of
causal sufficiency and is addressed instead to the radically different
notion of *rational purpose*. It is an answer to a why-type and not a

how-type question and it is largely indifferent to observable data. That is, theological propositions refer to a causal agency no matter what the actual observable facts of the world may be. They are not, then, *explanatory* but, as it were, justificatory and constitute what may be called *ultimate* justifications in that no other justification can be more fundamental.

It is not my intention to impose eccentric meanings on ordinary words and so I must qualify the conclusion according to which scientific explanations are "ultimate." Surely the theologian means to explain why things are as they are when referring to "the will of God" or "the divine plan" or "Providence." But such terms are after all indifferently applicable to nearly every or any natural phenomenon. Declaring an event to be consistent with or ordained by "the will of God" is not an explanation of the event as much as a moral conviction that the event *ought* to have occurred. There is no limit to the means available to an omnipotent being, and thus scientific laws may reveal just one of the ways an omnipotent will expresses itself. Regarded in this light, the theological account is more fundamental than the scientific for it at once includes the (scientific) explanation of *how* things come about and the justification for their being as they are.

I insert this otherwise digressive comparison to underscore the subtlety of questions regarding the "goodness" of explanations. We cannot assign values of goodness to any account until we are sure of the level at which we are attempting to understand the phenomena under consideration. It is at this point that the difference between vertical and horizontal generalizations (chapter 1) becomes especially relevant. Theological and scientific accounts are at different levels; the former at the level of justification where *sufficient reasons* are postulated and the latter at the level of explanation where *sufficient causes* are specified. Scientific accounts are nonevaluative—not "value-neutral" but *non*evaluative. Neutrality is a position between antagonistic alternatives. In the evaluative realm, scientific accounts have no position, including the neutral one.

With all due respect to ordinary language, therefore, I must point to the difference between explaining an event and giving a reason for it. We explain the voltage-drop in a circuit when we invoke Ohm's law and note that a resistance has just been inserted into the circuit. This, however, cannot be the *reason* for the voltage-drop, for rationality plays no part. It is convenient to use the terms "explanation" and "reason" interchangeably in many contexts, but it is also a source of confusion when we examine carefully the sorts of accounts the discipline of Psychology should strive to develop. Thus, the laws of sensory physiology may provide a good explanation for Smith's claim that a perceived light has grown in brightness but they do not provide a reason for Smith's choice of Impressionist over pre-Raphaelite paintings. Now, the likely response to this comparison is that aesthetic preferences involve more than sensory physiology; they involve prior learning, complex cognitive processes, various emotional factors. But this is really off the point. What is different about aesthetic preferences when compared with judged brightness is not the complexity of the former but the implicit justificatory argument needed to account for it. Even if it were shown that the preference is (somehow) causally determined by events in Smith's nervous system, we could still press on to establish whether there were good *reasons* for the preference, whatever its cause. It is because of this that the century-old search for mechanisms has distracted psychologists perhaps more than it has helped them.[11] This will become clearer as we review several genres of psychological explanation and attempt to determine if they are "good" ones. The concept of motivation will be used illustratively in the following sections.

Psychoanalytic Explanations

The argot of psychoanalytic theory has now been absorbed into the working vocabulary of the general public such that entirely theoretical terms function as if they were causal explanations. In chapter 2, in the context of the reasons-causes tension, I referred briefly to the oxymoronic nature of "unconscious motivation" and I shall now expand upon that preliminary judgment.

I should begin by noting the ambiguity surrounding

the concept of motivation itself. It has had a checkered history in Psychology. It has been used to refer to entirely biological processes,[12] to specific volitions,[13] to instinctive dispositions,[14] and to learned behavioral dispositions.[15] In some texts it is a species of "desire," in others a blind impulse of "drive." Suggestively, it is generally included with the topic of emotion in most introductory treatments, presumably because motives, like emotions, are "felt" and because they impel the organism toward or away from stimuli of a certain kind. In ordinary language, persons describe themselves as "motivated" when explaining the relish they take in one or another activity; i.e., as synonymous with "desirous" or "eager." Thus, in ordinary language the concept of motivation is distinguished from compulsion. One is not likely to say that he parted with his wallet because the thief "motivated" him. But the concept is also distinguished from whim or caprice. The utterance "I don't know why I did it" is typically reserved for actions for which a discernible motive cannot be found even by the agent. In common parlance, then, a motive is or at least is kindred to a *reason*. Thus, in common parlance, an *unconscious motive* is a contradiction in terms.

Learned disciplines are not, however, obliged to honor the linguistic conventions of the general public. Psychoanalysts may have good reasons for speaking of unconscious motives or for rejecting the common wisdom as regards the rough equivalence of motives and reasons. One good reason would be that such usage permits them to frame good explanations for events otherwise inexplicable. But a good explanation here is one grounded in causal sufficiency and appealing to nothing less than a law of science. It is one that specifies the initial conditions under which "unconscious motivation" invariably produces the behavior to be explained. To achieve this level of explanation, however, we are not permitted to include the causal element in the definition of the *explanandum*, for this would give us no more than a definitional truth of the *vis dormativa* variety. What is needed, therefore, is a basis upon which to classify a behavioral event as unconsciously motivated without smuggling unconscious motivation into the definition or description of the behavior.

Aggression or hostility is often cited as arising from unconscious motives. But, of course, aggression and hostility are often quite consciously directed toward others and for reasons well known to the person having these feelings. So far we can say that unconscious processes may be sufficient to produce the sentiment but not necessary. If they are to be productive of the sentiment they must arise from *repressed* feelings of which the experient is unaware. It turns out, then, that *repression* is a sufficient (and necessary?) condition for there to be unconsciously motivated aggression. But this then yields a sequence in which aggressive sentiments are sufficient for (later) aggressive sentiments! The middle stage of the sequence involves "repression" but there is no description or definition of this "process" that does not include the concept of the unconscious. It cannot be a test of the thesis for the thesis must be assumed in order for there to be "repression" at all. "Repression" is taken to be *purposive forgetting*—forgetting for a *reason*—but this implies either that the actor knows what he's forgetting (in which case it is not *unconscious*) or is forgetting for unconscious reasons. The latter, which is also oxymoronic, makes it impossible to define repression in any terms except those of unconscious processes; but repression is then regarded as one of the tests of just these processes.

Freud was persuaded that such difficulties would be removed by advances in the neural sciences such that the theory-terms of psychoanalysis would be replaced by the observation-terms of neurophysiology. But this is impossible. The neural sciences are correlative. They establish correlations between events in the nervous system and certain functions performed by persons or animals. We can speak intelligibly of the neural correlates of learning or memory or perception because learning, memory, and perception are publicly displayed by organisms satisfying empirical criteria. But we cannot verify psychoanalytic concepts through neurological measures since the former—at least when pertaining to the "unconscious"—do not satisfy empirical criteria. What makes one failure to recall a species of forgetting and another a species of repression is not something determined by events in the nervous system but by the theories we propose. We must first have a non-neural basis for the distinction before we can hunt about for neural correlates of each.

Let us return to the question of whether the psychoanalytic notion of unconscious motivation is a good explanation of a certain class of events such as forgetting, hostility, or slips of the tongue. The record now seems clear enough for us to take at least the provisional position that the notion of unconscious motivation cannot function as a determinative causal law and so does not provide a scientific explanation at all. Rather, it may provide a *justification* of the sort: Given what Smith has been exposed to in childhood and thereafter, and given the way that background has shaped Smith's perceptions of himself and others, *it is quite reasonable* to expect him to harbor feelings of hostility and resentment toward persons in authority. We should not be surprised to discover that persons with backgrounds similar to Smith's do not have such feelings, or that others with very different backgrounds do. We should not be surprised because the feelings themselves arise not from causal sequences of a purely natural-physical nature but from ideographic considerations in which the actor's autonomy plays a part. The psychoanalytic account is a story, a narrative, but not a scientific one. It is rather a historical narrative—something of a saga—which is "good" or less than good depending upon the contact it makes with the reader's own experiences and thoughts. We ask of such accounts only whether they make sense, recognizing that they are but one of an indefinite number of possible accounts all of which may make as much (or as little) sense. Where scientific theories are explanations of facts, psychoanalytic theories are, in a way, theories about theories. The patient has a theory: "I must have a reason for disliking Jones so much"; and the analyst has a theory too: "He reminds you of your father". In the course of therapy, this is all expanded and plumbed, the result being a dramatic recreation of the patient's life. In the end, the patient must decide how good the recreation is, but must do so without any standard of comparison. Thus, even the successful therapy may be just one of an indefinite number of equally successful ones, but for practical and personal purposes, one is enough!

The problem with psychoanalytic formulations is not that they are insufficiently "scientific" but that their defenders seek to install them as scientific at all. This is based upon a mistake as to just where such formulations fit in the scheme of understandings. They are not descriptive or explanatory but, ironically, rational and justificatory. I say ironically because of the murky *irrationalism* that psychoanalytic theory adopted from the first. But the appeal that psychoanalysis must make is ultimately to the patient's (and the critic's) rationality. The patient must discover that fears or feelings of a certain kind are not *justified*; they do not make intelligible contact with the current facts of the patient's life. In a word, they are the *wrong* fears or feelings now, no matter how understandable it is that they would initially come into being. Setting aside all the interpretive energies, all the symbology and hocus-pocus, the therapeutic setting becomes effective when the patient begins to recognize the depicted past as his own and thereupon begins to weigh prevailing sentiments and thoughts arising from the past against current facts and current possibilities. The patient on the mend is the one who knows the *reason* for, not the "cause" of the disturbance. If Freud's rather innocent hopes could have been realized such that a patient could be given a complete neurological record of all the events leading up to the current illness, the record would count as nothing toward the ultimate resolution of the dilemma. A knowledge of causes would be academic, scientific, nugatory. For the same reason, irrationalist accounts are therapeutically ineffective. They make no *sense* because they make no contact with events occurring at the level at which the patient's problems are found and felt.

By way of summary, I would say that psychoanalytic approaches to the concept of motivation are to be understood as rationalistic and justificatory, the latter in only a weak moral sense. Causal explanations in science are never justificatory in either a strong or a weak sense and are not *intelligible* in the way that rational accounts are. In light of this, traditional formulations of motivation in psychoanalytic writings are off the point when they are grounded in instinctive processes or putative biological mechanisms. In the nonscientific sense of explanation, the psychoanalytic explanation of human behavior is a "good" explanation in a way that a play has a good plot or a novel is credible or historical essays are intelligible. The sort of judgment brought to bear on accounts of this kind is of the form "It may very well have come about this way," not "It is true because it is an instance of a universal law," or "It was inevitable because it was determined by causally sufficient conditions."

As I have discussed at length in another context [16] this is but one of the reasons why such accounts have no place in the evidentiary phases of adjudication. A psychoanalytic account of felonious behavior is neither a scientific explanation nor a *moral* justification (in the strong sense) but a *rationalization* by which the facts of the crime become intelligibly connected to the biological and cognitive nuances of the defendant's life. Such accounts cannot establish that the crime was determined or irresistible or compelled; only that, "It may very well have come about that way." When all this is considered, we begin to appreciate the pointlessness of programs designed to translate psychoanalytic statements into scientific ones. The more credible and useful alternative is one in which concepts such as motivation are employed to render a story intelligible; to allow empathic responses from its auditors; to raise still other questions about other ways the same events might have come about or might have been resolved.

Mechanistic Explanations

Referring to the work of D. J. MacFarland, [17] Austen Clark notes that, "The idea that deviations from a physiologically optimal state actuate behavioural mechanisms controlled by negative feedback is very fruitful" (p. 58). [18] In the same passage Clark shows that this concept of negative feedback is at the center of many theories of motivation, including those advanced by E. C. Tolman, Clark Hull, Dalbir Bindra, and MacFarland himself. In the tradition made prominent by Hull, such theories are often called "drive-reduction" models of motivation in that they take motivation to

be equivalent to or operationally definable as a state of physiological disequilibrium. The behavior triggered by such states either
restores equilibrium and is thus "reinforcing" or does not. In the
latter instance, survival itself is in jeopardy. The successful organism, however, emits behavior that reduces or eliminates those
internal events or signals that led to the behavior itself. Here, then,
is the "negative feedback" component of a system designed to
minimize extreme devitations. Taking the actual behavior of food-
deprived or water-deprived animals, the theorist is then able to
construct an analytical model (and, in principle, a physical one
too) that predicts such events as rate or force of response under
specified conditions of deprivation, and one that is able also to
match the manner in which such behavior decreases as the system is restored to an equilibrium-state. Where thirst and starva-
tion are the sources of deviations within the system, "equilibrium" is roughly synonymous with "satiety." The question arising
from this interesting approach is whether such models provide a
good explanation of motivation; whether motivation is the sort of
condition or property suited to scientific explanation at all.

It is useful, if not unavoidable, to begin appraisals of
such models with the aid of introspection. Were we totally unaware of our own motives, there would be no known "problem of
motivation" for scientists and theorists to consider. Introspectively, however, there is no evidence of *physiological* disequilibrium,
only of experiences or sensations (hunger, thirst, pain) of a certain kind. The cause of Smith's eating may be physiological, but
the reason Smith eats is that he is hungry. In other words, the
cause of Smith's eating may not be Smith's cause. Accordingly, a
negative-feedback model of motivation may provide a good account of processes leading up to eating, but no account at all of
the basis upon which the respondent undertakes the activity or
answers the summons.

Mechanistic models of motivation may be interpreted
as "psychological" by implication, in that we might regard measures or degrees of disequilibrium as the observable correlates of
such introspectively known conditions as "hunger" and "thirst."
But if the authors of such models actually assume as much, the

models themselves are incomplete until there is some component or module included that has the function of awareness, feelings, and the like. What might make disequilibrium motivating is not simply its magnitude but its sensed or experienced magnitude. A model of the former that leaves no room for the latter is not, then, a model of motivation but of, for example, metabolism or digestion.

One might counter this by insisting that such models are good or bad only to the extent that they predict behavior under specified circumstances and, if they can do so without recourse to "psychic" processes, all the better. This, however, is an *ignoratio* fallacy since the question has to do with how well such models *explain* motivation and not with how accurately they predict behavior. The symmetry between explanation and prediction is preserved only through universal (covering) laws. A mechanistic model of motivation would explain motivation, therefore, only if its predictions were grounded in such a law or took it for granted from the first. But what, then, is the law? If it is a physiological law—to the effect that tissue-needs invariably create states of disequilibrium successfully reversed only by provision of nutrients—then we must wrestle with the fact that the nutritive value of a substance does not predict the behavior of food-deprived animals.[19]

As noted in the previous chapter, prediction and explanation are interchangeable only under rare circumstances. Evolutionary theory provides explanations of phenotypic variation but not predictions of them. Weather forecasting provides predictions of climatic conditions but not scientific explanations of them. Psychoanalytic explanations are retrodictive and are "explanatory" only in the sense previously discussed. It is not sufficient, therefore, to point to the predictive prowess of mechanistic accounts of motivation when the question is one of explanation. Moreover, what makes such models predictive is no more than what would make an empirical function predictive. Were we to plot response-rate as a function of hours of food-deprivation, and include as a parameter the percent of responses resulting in the delivery of food during postdeprivation trials, we would have the same predictive efficiency as that offered by any such model. The model, after all, is a model of the data, not the organism. We can appreciate its heuristic value without being misled by its scarcely coincidental predictive power. The latter is actually a veiled re-trodictive power supplied entirely by data already at hand.

When we move from the level of animal behavior, and specifically that which proceeds from appetitive motivations, and consider *human* motivation, mechanistic models of the sort noted above are even less plausible. The commoner forms of human motivation are assumed by defenders of mechanistic models (e.g., Hull) to arise from more "basic" drives such as those for food, water, and pain. Money, for example, is said to take on the prop-erties of a "secondary reinforcer" because of its reliable associa-tion with such "primary reinforcers" as food and shelter. Persons are then said to be "motivated" to work for money *via* a general-ization from one reinforcer to another or a learned substitution of one (the "primary") for the other (the "secondary"). What is not at all clear from such accounts is whether money, in this case, has the same drive-reducing powers as food and restores "equi-librium" in the way that food is alleged to when a hunger-drive exists. This seems intuitively to be nearly preposterous, for it would lead to the prediction that persons suddenly lose their appetites on payday! Kindred examples drawn from animal learning are no more plausible, even if less patently absurd. Models that require secondary-reinforcers to gain their efficacy by sharing in the drive-reducing properties of primary reinforcers contain no plausible causal or mechanistic element by which this sort of trade could take place. The chimp who works for tokens that activate a food-dispensing device surely is not treating the tokens as "reinforc-ing" in the way that food is, unless the chimp proceeds to eat the tokens. The tokens will not satisfy any tissue-need produced by food-deprivation. They may (as in the Hullian account) produce "anticipatory" responses—including visceral ones—but such an-ticipations are evidence of a means-end strategy or cognitive pro-cess which is not at all embraced by something as simple as "negative feedback." Such "anticipatory" states are an example of smuggled psychological terms in a model that would present it-self as purely mechanistic.

Then, too, the state of "satiety"—the psychological equilvalent of physiological "equilibrium"—is introduced only clumsily into a coherent and general theory of human motivation. Ordinary persons, called upon to list the chief motives of their lives and works, are inclined to offer objectives with which we do not become "satiated." Social beings are motivated to form friendships, to attain some success in their relationships with others, to conduct their affairs in a manner that is equitable and virtuous, to live in a state of harmony and justice. We surely do not have "enough harmony" or "enough friendship" in the sense that we have "enough water." Nor would we be inclined to over- look wickedness on the grounds that the perpetrator had, after all, been decent "long enough"! It just turns out that what fills the lists of human motives are entries entirely unlike the basic biological impulses routinely included in drive-reduction models of motivation.[20] The latter are exemplars only of members of the same genre and attempts at *vertical generalization* have the quality of drollery.

The theoretical ambiguities occur when we conflate the concepts of *drive* and *motivation* or treat the having of impulses as akin to the having of purposes, even where the latter are *pursued* impulsively. There is, for example, still much arbitrariness in def- initions of motivation even among those otherwise inclined to avoid mentalistic language. The term is sometimes (often) em- ployed to refer to a condition of the organism; sometimes to refer to a goal; sometimes to refer to an experimental operation; sometimes to refer to a preference for one of two or more stimuli. Nor is it clear that there is one general state of motivation that may be applied to any number of external "satisfiers," or a spe- cific motive for each external the animal will work to obtain or to avoid. The literature on frustration-effects points to any number of "substitute-gratifications" chosen by animals unable to reduce a "relevant drive"; but this is a literature that is rife with both implied and stated psychological terms and, as a result, ceases to qualify as a defense of mechanistic theories of motivation.[21]

Physical models of motivation, whether in the form of animals or block-diagrams or physically realized block-diagrams, are of value to the extent that they render more tractable the nagging problems posed by human motivation. Presumably, the appropriate strategy is one that begins with the more reliable facts of human motivation and then attempts to translate or model these in such a way as to provide at least conceptual control over those variables that are sufficient to yield versions of these facts. But the traditional strategy within mechanistic Psychology has been to ignore the most obvious and reliable facts of human motivation, and then to construct a model of the behavior of organisms of doubtful representativeness exposed to conditions of doubtful relevance. Success is then claimed when the model—which is devised in light of experimental findings—generates outputs similar to those obtained from the experimental subjects.

I should not close this section without pausing to examine the notion of "equilibrium" itself, which is at the core of many mechanistic models of motivation. It is not at all obvious that equilibrium-states are common in biological systems, or even desirable; nor do traditional drive-reduction theories specify just where in the system and in what manner the alleged equilibrium reveals itself. The very process of stimulation is disequilibrating only in relation to a resting-state which is no more normal or typical than a state of excitation. Recall that the ultimate "steady-state" is death, not tranquility. At the cellular level, the processes of learning and memory—which are presumably central to motivation—lead to structural synaptic changes and perhaps to recurrent patterns of excitations dramatically different from the state of the system prior to these acquisitions. Of course one might say that such processes represent new equilibrium-levels, but this renders the concept even more arbitrary and less distinguishable from whatever it is that equilibrium is to be contrasted with. Thus, notions such as "dynamic equilibrium" are empty when applied to complex organisms since, for such organisms, there can be no "static equilibrium" as long as life endures. The metabolic physiology of organisms includes anabolic and even morbid components, for the processes of growth and physiological maintenance are earned at a price. To speak in recognizable physiological terms, we should contrast not "equilibrium" and "disequilibrium," but *normal* and *pathological*, where the latter refers to identifiable physiological changes of sufficient magnitude to produce either the death of the organism or a permanent dysfunction of one of its systems. But this meaningful distinction then makes improbable any useful connection with the facts of motivation and these significant physiological changes. Long before we reach the level of human beings, we will discover motivated behavior bearing no relationship to biological survival *per se*, except for relationships that beg the very question at issue. The primate that avoids food in order to peer through a small window to observe other animals or human beings is scarcely the model of a motivational system secured to considerations of survival.[22] There is no doubt but that animals behave in such a way as to enhance the probability of continued life. By virtue of reflexive and instinctive patterns of behavior, such adaptations become possible even in the absence of training, coaxing, or conditioning. The behavior is impelled or driven by factors relatively independent of reinforcement histories or, at the human level, deliberation and choice. But since we already know that the more important human motivations are inextricably connected to deliberation and choice, we have reason to wonder whether such reflexive and instinctive patterns are apt models of human motivation. There is good reason to think that by far the better model is one in which the animal too acts on the advantages of prior experience and memory; that is, where the animal's "motives" are acquired and not plausibly construed as either reflexive or instinctive. But, as noted, the behavior associated with acquired motives is often so removed from considerations of survival as to have practically no relationship to it at all.

Are mechanistic explanations of motivation good ones? Unlike psychoanalytic accounts, they hold out the promise of being explanations, for they make appeal directly to causally sufficient (scientific) laws. The problem, however, is that they do not appear to be (scientific) explanations of motivation *qua* motivation, at least as studies of *human* motivation give meaning to the term. Mechanistic explanations would seem to be versions of physiological laws or tendencies or mere restatements of them. In the form of models, the explanations are of data, not organisms or their physiologies.

Teleological Explanations

The general public understands the concept of motivation teleologically and in this has the support of humanistic psychologists, rigorous and otherwise.[23] To say that Smith is motivated is to say that Smith has a goal or purpose and is acting in such a way as to attain it. Smith's behavior is understood in light of Smith's purposes, these taken to be synonymous with Smith's "motives." The advantage of teleological explanation is obvious: It conforms perfectly with a common sense not paralyzed by the refinements of analysis. The disadvantages are also obvious: There is an irritating circularity in the definitions of "motivations" and "goals," not to mention the reckless anthropomorphism encouraged by the "goal-directed" behavior of infrahuman organisms. Perhaps worst of all, however, is the status given to Smith in this matter for, on the common sense account, only Smith can truly know his own motives (*pace* Freud).

Teleological accounts are not, however, univocal. An entity may act *for* a purpose without acting *with* a purpose; e.g., a carrier pigeon with a note tied to its leg. An entity may attain a goal serendipitously so that, although there was a purpose, the behavior that attained it did so by accident or inadvertence. Evolutionary theory is teleological in the sense that phenotypes are "selected" for survival; e.g., some male birds have plummage that is sexually exciting to female members of the species and this *so that* there will be copulation. But evolutionary theory is not teleological in the sense that an intending agent must be assumed for the selections to occur. Psychoanalytic theory is also teleological in this respect, in that it treats unconscious motivation as serving a purpose but does not attribute to the patient any conscious or intentional part. What is common to the evolutionary and the psychoanalytic accounts is the elimination of autonomy on the part of participants whose behavior nevertheless serves some purpose judged to be vital. Having discussed autonomy at length in chapter 2, it is enough to say here that this elimination renders both evolutionary theory and psychoanalytic theory largely irrelevant to the issue of human motivation. If Smith has "repressed" a thought or feeling, such that he has no conscious awareness of it, then although the allegedly repressed material may motivate Smith, it cannot be Smith's motive. More generally, to the extent that his behavior is impelled (as, for example, by the laws of mechanics), it does not proceed from *Smith's* motives.

This is not averted by reducing Smith's motives to some state or condition of Smith's brain or body (cf. chapter 3), for what is under consideration here is the basis upon which Smith understands himself to be behaving. He does not know that hypothalamic nuclei are active, but that he is hungry; he does not know that a tumor is invading structures in the limbic system, but that he is anxious. The bodily conditions may be the *cause* of this or that psychological state but cannot be the *reason* why Smith does X or Y when in this state. As every idea is someone's, so too every reason is someone's.

It is because of this that the evolutionary account fails as totally as the psychoanalytic. There may be some physical basis on which John is drawn to Mary; a basis regulated by genetically governed reflexes and instincts selected over the eons to favor heterosexual pairings. To this extent, the attractive forces are indifferent to any given pairing, including that of John and Mary. But this cannot be *John's* motive, since he, as it happens, left school in the third grade and has never heard either of genes or of the theory of evolution. We might want to say at this point that John is just ignorant of the "real" source of the attraction, but this is tantamount to saying that John is acting on the wrong motive. However, how can one act on the wrong motive? It makes sense to say that, given motive-X, action-A will not satisfy it; e.g., the hungry rat runs toward a drinking-tube rather than a food-well. But it makes no sense to say that the motive to eat is the wrong one. As with his aches and pains, Smith has the last word on his motives. And his motives turn out to be different from anything occurring at the level of his genes, his olfactory tract, or his limbic system.

The teleological approach to human motivation cannot be usefully removed from the introspective domain in which actual persons attempt to identify just what goal or objective it is to which their behavior is functionally and intelligibly related. Thus, the approach when properly made does not promise a scientific explanation of motives but, again, a *rationalization* of them. I would judge it to be the soundest approach if only because it is the only one that is not transparently irrelevant. It carries the now grave liability of not fitting comfortably into the laboratory, though it may in fact contain observational possibilities rather more rigorous than mere gossip.

Most will agree, I should think, that the more important sources of human motivation are those tied to social contexts in which the feelings, judgments, and expectations of others count in the formation of personal goals. Alternatives to the teleological approach would seem to be especially implausible in these contexts. As Peter Winch argued so successfully years ago,[24] mechanistic and reductionistic programs in the *social* sciences are unintelligible or illicit. They suffer the latter fate when essentially social constructs are imported into our mechanistic vocabulary. To "reduce" interactions among persons to something nonsocial requires first the translation of "interactions" into some nonsocial alternative. Winch's point, stated all too briefly here, is that there are minimal criteria by which an event is recognizable as a *social* event; to erect a barrier against the inclusion of these criteria is not finally to explain social phenomena but to deny their occurrence. Collingwood[25] made the same case in the matter of historical events, as did Hegel earlier[26] and William Dray later.[27] Only recently, through research and theory in the area of social cognition,[28] has Psychology more fully respected the implicitly propositional nature of social interactions; interactions that combine persons with unique and quasi-theoretical positions regarding the motives, character, attributes and perceptions of their cohorts. Social interactions take place *for a purpose* and are regulated, if that is the right word, by the mixture of purposes and beliefs each member brings to the social context. I would prefer to state the point in a way that makes such activities seem less conspiratorial, but here I pass on only the flavor of an important if still too *scientistic* literature. What makes it important is surely not that discovery of the obvious which besets Psychology when it agrees to address life beyond the laboratory. Rather, the literature is important because it is gradually uncovering sound and replicable methods for isolating what are often very subtle but significant aspects of social interaction. Some of what is now routinely reported was never obvious; and much that is obvious is now becoming systematic rather than merely anecdotal. Yet, the best of this literature is teleological from start to finish, even if this element is concealed by *journalese*. Predictably, the accounts are primarily *narrative*, for all the statistics, and invite the reader to establish an essentially empathic relationship with the nameless persons behind the findings. What we receive, therefore, is not a causal explanation in the scientific sense but, again, a species of rationalization.

It may seem, in light of the repeatability of such studies, that this designation does not fit; that here, at least, we do have a scientific explanation for here at least there is prediction, precision, and lawfulness. There are, indeed, these three, but the lawfulness is not *causal* in the sense developed in chapter 2. It is because persons enter social contexts with rationally articulated objectives and with rationally defended beliefs or attitudes that we are able to predict how they are likely to react to disconfirming evidence or to obstacles denying ready access to their goals. That is, it is because they are rational that their reactions can be lawfully described and predicted. Note that I am not claiming that their attitudes or beliefs are, in the abstract, "rational"; only that their defense of them takes a rationalized form. The important factor is the participants' overarching goal to render their attitudes and beliefs conformable to the dictates of rationality or intelligibility. Presumably, they could at any point suspend this commitment or even commit themselves to pure caprice. Were this to occur, the generalizations contained in this literature would be overturned and the studies themselves would be entirely unreplicable. Rationalized beliefs, perceptions, and attitudes are fundamental to *social* phenomena and are recovered in any careful study of such phenomena.

That the bishop will only be moved diagonally in a game of chess can be predicted with certainty, assuming both players are playing chess. What confers predictive efficiency in this case is not a law of science or causal determination, but the Rules of Chess combined with the stipulation that no one plays chess except according to the rules. Persons having the strong conviction that the world's end is imminent are inclined to admit that they got the date wrong when the earth is still intact, but they do not surrender the belief. What we have in such instances is just another way of describing what it means to have a *conviction* as opposed, for example, to a scientific hypothesis or a mere opinion. Our ability to predict how those with strong convictions will react to disconfirming evidence is tied to the very meaning of *a strong conviction* and to the tools of rationalization available to rational beings faced with such a dilemma. We mustn't make too much (or too little) of the social psychologist's success in predicting such outcomes. We would make too much of it if we assumed that prediction was grounded in causal laws; too little if we assumed that only the obvious or the trivial had been (re-)discovered. The fair and profitable assessment is that such research points clearly to the centrality of teleological factors in any systematic account of social phenomena. Social beings who strive for consistency, or labor to reconcile their convictions to the facts, or form attitudes by which to diminish the complexity of social interactions, or bring their judgments into line with those of a group or with those in authority are doing these things with an end in view.[29] Pressed to defend any of these strivings, they will offer a rational account in which purposes form an integral part. They may not know the particular pressures they're giving in to and may not even know all of the devices (cognitive, attentional, affective) employed in behalf of these purposes. But in the very act of rationalizing their positions they disclose an aspect of themselves that is intelligible only on teleological or purposive grounds.

Are There Good Explanations in Psychology?

Consider the area of social Psychology refereed to as *attribution theory*,[30] which in broad terms is concerned with how persons arrive at understandings of the conduct of others. Let us say that we are observing a game of chess at a distance and, after a time, notice that one of the players no longer moves the Bishop diagonally but now begins to move it vertically and horizontally. Studies of attribution indicate that in such circumstances we are inclined to understand the earlier conduct as *externally* controlled (here, by the rules of chess), but the later conduct as arising from something *internal* in the player; something amiss or even reproachable. We might be inclined to say that a condition of amnesia set in during the game, or that the players's visual perception had become untrustworthy, or even that the wrong moves were inspired by a scheme to take unfair advantage of the opponent. Now, suppose our question is, "Why do observers look to blame players making wrong moves, but attribute the correct ones to factors external to the players?" And suppose the answer is of this general form: *When we attempt to account for the behavior of others, we actually perform a kind of hypothesis-testing. If external causes are sufficient to account for the behavior, we settle for a kind of causal account but where they are not we are inclined to attribute the actor with (internal) private motives or states of a praiseworthy or blameworthy nature.* What sort of explanation is this, and is it a good one?

Clearly, it is not a *nomological-deductive* explanation for no universal law is known to cover such effects which are, after all, only tendencies in any case. Nor is it a *reductive* explanation for none of the psychological terms has been reduced to nonpsychological or physical ones. It is, in fact, a *teleological* explanation because it is tied to the assumption, if only implicit, that observers are striving to understand the behavior of others and, in the process, will construct and test one theory after another until they have one that makes the behavior in question intelligible. Just as the observers are attempting to locate the behavior within a rational (rationalized) context, so also are the experimenters and theoreticians trying to rationalize the observed performance of the observers.

Whether we judge the attribution literature as presenting good explanations or not depends in the last analysis on our *empathic* reactions to such accounts. We are—like the observers themselves—trying to make sense of the explanation by asking ourselves if it would cover our own judgments had we been the observers. One who reads articles in this vein must ask, "Is this the sort of logic I follow when faced with conduct by others that is not clearly explicable in terms of external constraints?" Let us take a case where a new Soviet president declares a policy of nuclear disarmament at about the same time as a similar proposal is made by the President of the United States. We might discover that many Americans would explain the U.S. policy as inspired by pacifism and the Soviet policy as arising from fear or duplicity. Social psychologists could explain these different attributions as grounded in traditional beliefs about the motives of the two nations; beliefs that now can be consistently held only by ascribing radically different motives to political leaders who have advanced the same proposal. This is a good explanation only from the essentially *introspective* perspective of those weighing it. We ask whether it conforms to those relationships between belief and attribution common to our own experiences.

It is not uncommon for critics of the social sciences to dismiss such explanations as obvious, trivial, and unscientific, but the criticism is derived from flawed expectations as to what such "sciences" have as a plausible and defensible objective. Their findings and explanations are not always "obvious" and are often far from trivial. The apparent obviousness is conveyed by what is finally the *rationality* of the accounts and not any *a priori* certainties we have as to what the findings will be. Thus, the literature addressed to *attribution theory*, for example, is "obvious" to the disinterested critic because, after weighing it, the critic finds it to be *obviously true* or at least obviously true in many cases. No one seriously avers that, "Well, now that I think about it, force really is equal to the product of mass and acceleration." But it is only after we think about it that, indeed, we see how our own attributions are often rooted in the implicit logic guiding the experimental subjects studied by the social psychologists. The theory and research are not scientific, but not for reasons of carelessness or incompetence or ignorance. They are not scientific chiefly because they have been stripped of the element of causal necessitation which *prima facie* just has nothing to do with the phenomena of interest.

It is only because work in such areas is conducted within an experimental framework that we often have the flawed expectation of genuinely scientific explanations. But the "experiments" come closer to a kind of controlled interview than to an assessment of truly causal dependencies. In recording the utterances of the subjects, the psychologist in such settings takes for granted their autonomy, authenticity, rationality, intentions, and the like. These nonscientific factors fail to appear in the experimental design or in the data not because they have been "controlled" or eliminated, but because they constitute the very context—the necessary assumptions—for the research questions to be framed and addressed.

The explanations forthcoming are good because they are reasonable. Their reasonableness is earned by way of an introspective test to which scientific explanations are never properly submitted. It is only by the same test that such characterizations as obviousness or triviality could be applied.

What, then, of other psychological explanations? I should think the same test is applicable to all of them; the test of reasonableness, of introspective plausibility, of empathic evocativeness. I do not legislate here on the activities of psychologists or the kinds of statements they must strive to make. The psychologist who is interested in (probably causal) relationships between hypothalamic lesions and food-consumption is free to explore them, as long as we recognize that the results are not to be taken as a causal explanation of *hunger as a motive*. The results are better assigned to scientific knowledge about the physiology of appetitive behavior than to psychological knowledge about the nature of human motivation. There is room for argument on both sides of the issue and there are, no doubt, hard cases each side would have difficulty accommodating. Reasonableness and plausibility are ultimate but not exclusive criteria of psychological explanations. The point is that they are not criteria at all of scientific explanation when they are taken as arising from irreducibly introspective sources.

I should repeat cautions given throughout this chapter. I am not proposing that the word "explanation" be reserved exclusively for nomological-deductive accounts unless the explanation is offered as a scientific one. Obviously, there are good explanations that are not scientific. What I have attempted to develop is a provisional taxonomy of explanations as well as arguments as to where within this taxonomy psychological accounts most defensibly fall. There are strong reasons for being wary as to the place of the nomological-deductive model itself, even within the sciences. What critics of the model have not accomplished, in my view, is an alternative that is as inclusive, exclusive and coherent. Such alternatives as the functional one discussed in the previous chapter and the teleological one in the present chapter leave too much to be desired. Functional explanations with any predictive power at all rest on empirical laws of sufficient reliability to qualify as explanation-sketches and to suggest the operation of more basic laws of a genuinely nomic variety. To state the case briefly, functional explanations are less alternatives to than incomplete species of nomological-deductive explanations.

Teleological accounts with psychological states and processes removed are not credible or even intelligible in their treatment of the sorts of phenomena in which Psychology traditionally and currently takes interest. And with the psychological dimension preserved, these same accounts are largely indistinguishable from the rationalized and narrative accounts found in historical scholarship, in ordinary common-sense explanations, and in literature.

CHAPTER FIVE

Ethics and Psychological Inquiry

The present chapter may appear at first to be incongruous in light of preceding pages, but there are at least three justifications for it. First, there are points of contact between Ethics and Psychology that are not found in the sciences in general. A fuller appreciation of the philosophical character of Psychology is thus cultivated by an examination of these points of contact. Secondly, the subject-matter of Ethics arises from certain facts of human nature. To the extent that this subject-matter is regarded as significant, we must inquire into the degree to which Psychology may help to explain it. Finally, psychological research and practice carry certain ethical burdens whose implications are too often ignored or lightly treated. A book devoted, as this one is, to the philosophical dimensions of Psychology has as one main objective the encouragement of debate on matters casually regarded as settled or irrelevant. There are ethical matters that have, alas, not been settled and that are by no means irrelevant either to the practice of Psychology or to an understanding of its essential nature. It is not accidental that both Ethics and Psychology, just a century ago, tended to be paired under the general heading *Moral Science*, and that leading texts regularly treated the ethical and psychological dimensions of human nature as mutually elucidating.[1] Jean Piaget[2] earlier in this century and Lawrence Kohlberg[3] at the present time are but two examples of psychologists who have productively explored the connection. But the numbers remain small, even as the influence of Psychology on ethical and political thought increases.[4]

It is surely not my intention within the limited space of a single chapter to touch upon, let alone closely examine, all of the points of contact between Psychology and Ethics. Nor, in the same space, can a critical exegesis of ethical theory be developed. Instead, the present chapter is offered as an illustration of the bearing these subjects have on each other; an illustration based upon only a few selected topics of sufficient generality to invite attention to the full range of interactions. In choosing representative and suggestive topics, there is a certain barrier to thematic integrity; a certain *ad hoc* character imparted to the chapter and likely to be distracting. I alert readers to this and encourage them to take each section as more or less independent of the others, even where overarching ethical principles are cited or implicitly assumed.

Science, Psychology, and Values

Whether or not Thomas Kuhn's account of scientific revolutions is sound, there has surely been something of a *Kuhnian* revolution in the social sciences since the appearance of his influential book.[5] Many psychologists have adopted an essentially Kuhnian position on Psychology, and regard its methods, subjects and guiding principles as "relative" to ever-shifting cultural and historical norms. There is now a quite general skepticism toward "absolutes" in any field of inquiry, including the physical sciences. Where the social sciences once and defensively insisted they were "value-neutral," they now tend to present themselves as unavoidably "value-loaded"; but in a way common to all scientific and intellectual pursuits.[6] Marxist or quasi-Marxist interpretations of the scientific enterprise find renewed vigor when apparent class-considerations seem to be at the bottom of fraudulent scientific reports.[7] But even when a specific ideological perspective is unuttered, psychologists and sociologists generally agree that science, as a human and social activity, can never sanitize itself against the intrusion of private or public aspirations, biases, and enthusiasms. This allegation is not confined to the social sciences themselves, but is stretched to embrace all of science. It is a "We're-no-worse-than-anybody-else" thesis when it is not a kind of fatalistic solipsism. But is it true? Rather, does it *claim* to be true? For if the thesis is a species of *claimed truth* then it makes appeal to standards of truth denied by the thesis itself. We begin to see, therefore, that this "sociology of knowledge" is not settled enough to be taken for granted as we attempt to comprehend the essential nature of scientific inquiry. It is not a datum but a theory. Actually, it is a theory of knowledge in that it sets limits on the objectivity and absoluteness of every knowledge-claim, including any coming from science. But it is a very complex and disorderly theory whose assets and defects are not easily discerned until the theory itself is dissected.

What does it mean to say that a scientist's own values or those of the reigning culture are inextricably bound up with the scientific activity itself? Certainly a scientist brings his or her values to the laboratory in the same way as aches and pains too are brought to the laboratory. But the sociological thesis does not rest on mere coincidences. What the thesis asserts is not that scientists, in possession of values, are the embodiment of these values wherever they happen to be; rather, the values *as values* affect the scientific undertaking itself. The proposed relationship is akin to having a toothache and going to the dentist. Our values ("value-structure") must be taken into account in any explanation of what scientists do as scientists.

Understood in this light, the thesis is provocative and rich in implications. Still, we must be clear on how the concept of "values" is meant to be taken, and where in the various stages of scientific activity its (alleged) influences are to be found. It may be true, for example, but only trivially so that Dr. Smith values antiques and does scientific research so that there is more disposable income to use for such "valuables." Dr. Jones, on the other hand, values the collegial friendships arising from teamwork in the laboratory and is committed to science chiefly because of this benefit. Dr. Brown, however, is a pathologically misanthropic cad whose research is designed to prove that human beings are natively wicked and can only be managed by ruthless means. In all three instances the "values" of the scientists inform us of the motivations or purposes that are to be satisfied by scientific labor, but in none of the three does the motivational fact describe or explain the work actually done once the scientist enters the laboratory. Indeed, the three scientists may actually be working on the same problem, may be using the same methods and may obtain the same results which they proceed to publish in very nearly the same form. Are we to understand, according to the sociological thesis, that our position on these published reports should be reserved until we learn which motives stood behind the efforts of each of the contributors?

The most celebrated case used to defend such a conclusion is that of Cyril Burt.[8] During a long and productive career, Burt became one of Britain's most eminent psychologists and had much to do with the use of psychological tests in pre-college education. He was, too, a committed hereditarian, fortified by his own research and that of others in the belief that genetic factors were chiefly responsible for variations in academic and socioeconomic achievement.

A measure of his prominence is given by the fact of his knighthood. Thus, when a good case for fraud on Sir Cyril's part was presented shortly after his death, a veritable growth-industry was spawned to deal with the scandal. It soon became clear that a number of Burt's papers included either illicit manipulations of the data or reported "data" which Burt had simply invented. Articles published over a period of years and describing entirely different samples included correlations identical to the third place after the decimal ($r = 0.771$). Articles also included the names of co-authors whose existence could not be established even after the broadest publicity. Some of the more influential papers appeared in a leading journal under Burt's own editorship despite their serious deficiencies in presenting the method of research and the details of the tested samples. Speculation on why Burt resorted to such techniques has been energetic. Perhaps the most plausible thesis is that Burt was sure of the general hereditarian conclusions and patched some articles together to revive interest in them during years when radical environmentalism was the reigning social philosophy.[9] In the interest of fairness, and in the face of formidable if circumstantial evidence to the contrary, we must also leave room for the possibility that his named co-authors did, in fact, work with him but are now nowhere to be found and that simple sloppiness was behind his reported correlations.

But Burt's motives and even his guilt are not central to the present discussion. Rather, he is offered as illustrative of a scientific personage whose social and personal attributes become thoroughly entangled with what he would have the public take to be a value-free scientific program. Even the defenders of the sociological theory of science will grant that cases such as this are rare, but will insist that they represent the extremity of a continuum on which all of science, all of human endeavor, must be located. Thus, if the Burt affair proves to be irrelevant or unable to sustain this thesis, we can be reasonably sure that the thesis itself is defective.

Actually, the thesis is somewhat mixed in its implications. In some form, it requires that we recognize even the conclusions of science to be value-loaded; in weaker forms, only that we understand the larger social context to which science and scientists are answerable and to some degree obedient. The strong version of the thesis can, I think, be dismissed rather readily. Whether or not intellectual capacities are highly heritable either is or is not a scientific question, which is to say a question that can only be settled by specific observations mandated by a rigorous theoretical framing of the proposition. Heritability (h^2), as it is usefully measured and manipulated in agronomy and animal husbandry, cannot be directly applied to settings in which there is uncontrolled and largely "open" breeding. There are, therefore, very substantial arguments against the possibility of obtaining valid measures of h^2 in human populations, at least with respect to complex phenotypes. This is not the place to consider the details of the scientific and technical issues. It is sufficient to say that hereditarians, including Cyril Burt, have been overly confident about the practical means by which biogenetic analysis and population genetics might be applied to this issue. Note, however, that a judgment in this area is grounded *exclusively* in statistical and genetic principles that are entirely independent of personal ideologies, social penchants and governmental policies.

The same, however, cannot be said of attempts to specify those phenotypes that go into making up "intelligence" or "mental ability" or, for that matter, "academic achievement." When h^2 is computed in agronomy and husbandry, the phenotypes are measurable in relatively straightforward and physical ways; e.g., the average height of crops, the average adult weight of litters, the ratio of fat to muscle, the average size of litters. The mental or cognitive dimensions of human psychology do not admit of such straightforward measurement or of such unarguable specification. The validity of mental tests typically rests upon the predictive efficiency they display in relation to performance in realistic settings. We would doubt the validity of a test of intelligence if scores earned by those taking it were entirely uncorrelated with intellectual accomplishments. It is here, of course, that a vicious circularity intrudes itself, for the very notion of "intellectual accomplishment" is intelligible only within a cultural context. Defenders of psychometric evaluations of this sort would serve their own interests better if they simply acknowledged this fact and offered no more than a shortcut technique for assessing "culturally specified intelligence."

But let us not make too much of this. The standard tests of mental ability consist of sections devoted to calculational agility, verbal fluency, inductive and deductive reasoning, and a general knowledge of salient features of the history of civilization, including politics, art, and literature. To say that such matters are culturally "relative" is to suggest that there might be a worthy and attractive "culture" even where no premium whatever is placed

upon such capacities. Well, perhaps there may be in some abstract sense a place so constituted. But how could it be *judged* as
worthy (by us or by the indigenous population) unless there were
sufficient expressivity in the local language and sufficient famil-
iarity with qualitative and quantitative scaling and with valid modes
of reasoning? I say we are not to make too much of the generous
concession to the effect that standard I.Q. tests are value-laden.
The "value" they are thus burdened by is one that has been
adopted by every definable culture, East and West, throughout the
recorded history of *Homo sapiens*. What is valued and what has been
valued is the ability to perform mental operations by which communication, measurement, reasoning, and strategies might be
shared with others or used for constructive personal purposes.
Again, the point here is that we can identify the part of the issue
that is "sociological" and we can also establish criteria by which
even this part might be assessed. Thus, even where the sociological considerations are uppermost, we are still not abandoned to
mere caprice, hopeless relativism, and the like. We can get a fairly
good "fix" on the performances that are essential if mental ability
is properly said to be abundant or limited or average, and we have
noncapricious ways of determining the (statistical) relationship
between measures of this ability and measures of successful performance in relevant contexts such as the classroom, the office
and the factory. We may reject, therefore, any argument to the effect that the resulting data are not only loaded with implicit values, but that we have no way of extricating the objective elements from the evaluative ones. Whether a pound of beef costs
$3.75 or 60 sea shells or a third of an elephant's tusk, the child
in these different economies who knows that two pounds cost $7.50
or 120 sea shells or two-thirds of a tusk knows something and
can do something unavailable to the children who don't. It is one
thing to say that culture-X "values" mathematical prowess, whereas
culture-Y doesn't. It is quite another to say that, because of this
relativity of values, we can't be absolutists on whether $7.50 is
twice $3.75!

It would not be fair to blame Thomas Kuhn for relativistic excesses, for he has generally agreed[10] that the sociolog-

ical elements in science tend to be marginal where the science itself is developed. For the latter he gives us a perhaps too "tribal" image of the scientific community thus insulated from external and social pressures but, if only as a historical account, his view seems sound. Theoretical Physics is obviously not as vulnerable to popular whims as is Sociology or Psychology. But Kuhn and his disciples have not, it would seem, traced out the implications of this fact. Physicists, as the phrase has it, are people too. Their resistance to external social pressures is not to be understood in psychological terms but in terms of the *scientific* coherence relating the facts, theories, and methods of Physics. It is simply false that sociological factors necessarily infect science (because they infect scientists), or that scientific pronouncements invariably express the "(relative)" values of a culture or subculture. It is false because it is contradictory when properly analyzed. To the extent that it purports to be a statement of fact, it must submit itself to standards of proof, but in so doing would implicitly deny the conclusion of the statement. To the extent that it purports to be an assertion of logical necessity, its falsity is established by the fact that a statement of the form "Scientific Law-X is true in all possible worlds" is not self-contradictory.

Adult persons the world over are known to engage in activities that require perception, memory, reasoning, and symbolic modes of communication. We take these to be "mental" processes or, on the mechanistic construal, "neural" processes. There is not now and never has been a known culture in which the categories of "correct" and "incorrect" have not been available and applied to these same processes. Some persons within a given culture will be right more often than others within the same culture. To a first approximation, therefore, we can say that in any numerous sample there will be variation in the performances of these and related tasks. Presumably, there is a test capable of disclosing the variation. In the abstract—and setting aside technical matters—we can ask the extent to which the measured variance is attributable to genetic variations within the sample. Putting the question with proper scientific and theoretical modesty, we can at least *wonder* how this measured variation might have differed had every person in the sample the same genetic composition as every other. There may be sound reasons for concluding that such a question could never be settled empirically; or that the public policies established for this culture should be indifferent to the results; or that some other challenge might come to face this culture and that the low-scoring members would be more fit to meet it; or that environmental interactions with genotypes are so complex and numerous that any conceivable result would be largely uninterpretable. These are all serious reservations and, in the last analysis, conclusive. But they are not supportive of the sociological thesis and in fact they combine to refute it. The reservations themselves can be segregated into scientific, social, and technical categories, and the principles of segregation will be accepted by competent scholars no matter what their ideologies might be. If this weren't so, Burt would not have had to lie, if he did. For there to be fraud, there must be a standard of identification; there must be a genuine dollar bill for there to be a counterfeit.

In chapter 2 scientific laws were presented as statements that *limit possibilities*, and this is an apt context for inserting this feature. In general, the room made available for values within an otherwise scientific endeavor is just what is left over when scientific laws have been included in the same space. What renders Physics immune to smuggled values, when it is immune, is not something unique to the methods or the language of the discipline. The immunity is conferred by scientific laws and by the logical connectives and formal rules of inference getting us from one set of laws to another. Psychology in the main is not in possession of such laws and, as argued in the preceding chapters, is not likely to be. Thus, Psychology and kindred disciplines cannot avoid the infusion of values in their general discourse, though they can in the purely quantitative mission of data-gathering and analysis. But the data-gathering proceeds from a question, and the question typically expresses at least an implicit evaluation of what is important to psychological beings and to relationships between them. There is, then, a value-fact compound in the social sciences that does not occur as uniformly and ineradicably in the natural sciences. Here, then, is but another criterion by which to recognize the formal difference between the two.

Ethical Values

It is another feature of the awkward manner in which the social sciences approach the issue of values that entirely dissimilar concepts are lumped together and treated as if there were no defensible way of distinguishing among them. Thus, the scientific enterprise is alleged to be value-laden or value-neutral depending upon the presence of (a) opinions, (b) merely personal inclinations or biases, (c) ethical presuppositions, (d) debatable professional estimations of significance, (e) veiled or explicit political or social agendas, or even (f) theoretical preferences.

Part of the problem is the equivocality of the word "value" which may refer to an abstract ethical canon; or merely a desirable attribute; or the price the market sets on a specific and material object; or a description of personal sentiments attached to an issue or action or thing. Thus, one may be said to value a friend, or to have got a good value for the price, or to recognize truth as a value or to assign higher value to a good book than to a good painting. These are, of course, incommensurable uses of the word and not all of them can be applied indifferently. To say, for example, that science is "value-neutral" cannot be to refer to (c), for the establishment of science is not only devoted to truth but actually depends for its very survival on the commitment to truth by its practitioners. It is, indeed, the central ethical presupposition of science that truth is preferred to falsehood and is to be pursued for its own sake. What sort of enterprise would science be were it not "laden" with this value?

What must be meant by those who would affirm or deny the neutrality of science in the matter of values is that science *qua* science places no stock in (a), (b), and (e) above, and makes provision for (d) and (f) only to the extent that these further the cause of science. Science does not "value" opinion or purely personal biases, nor does it tailor its discoveries to fit the prevailing political or social agenda. Unavoidably, scientists must decide what sort of science is worth doing and must proceed in their work within some sort of theoretical framework. The choice of topics and the wager placed on theories are governed by evaluative and not merely empirical considerations. They will be colored by eccentricities and hunches, and will often be forcefully shaped by establishmentarian mentalities. Nobody's perfect! But if this is all that is meant by "value-laden," the term is scarcely a reproach and is scarcely something the scientific community should or even can avoid.

Where the issue arises is at the point scientists *externalize* either the evaluative elements that are indispensable to scientific work or *internalize* those otherwise commendable social and political values which are, nonetheless, irrelevant or even damaging to the scientific enterprise. In the first instance, what is a useful finding highly productive of illuminating research is offered to the public as equally useful for settling matters that are nonscientific in the first instance. More generally, this externalization takes the form of requiring nonscientific issues to be determined according to standards that are appropriate only to science itself. We witness this unwarranted and often impertinent externalization in a growing number and variety of settings, typically for purposes of advocacy. I will turn to this in the next section. Internalization is in evidence when scientists choose questions and topics on the basis of social trends or governmental interests, or when the essential nature of the scientific endeavor is apologetical. The Burt affair turned up its share of quasi-scientific publications in which social values and policies were internalized by the factions within the scientific community.[11]

Genuinely ethical or moral values function in a manner similar to that displayed by genuinely scientific laws. And ethical or moral arguments are of the same form as the nomological-deductive arguments of the established sciences. Note that what is asserted here is that the *functions* and the *forms* are similar, not the content and not the criteria of truth. As with "covering laws," so too are moral premises universalized. Granting the validity or truth of a univesal moral premise, the conclusion of a moral argument is deductively certain once the (factual) minor premise is supplied. The symmetry may be thus illustrated:

MORAL (RATIONAL) EXPLANATION	SCIENTIFIC (CAUSAL) EXPLANATION
1. It is universally obligatory that X.	1. It is universally determined that X.
2. Action-Y is a species of X.	2. Event-Y is an instance of X.
3. Necessarily, Y is obligatory.	3. Necessarily, Y occurs.

If, for example, the major moral premise is that it is universally wrong to take the life of an innocent and nonthreatening human being, necessarily it is wrong to take the life of Smith *if* Smith is an innocent and nonthreatening human being. As with nomological-deductive explanations, the coverage of universalized moral premises may be limited by various and specified initial or boundary conditions. And as with nomological-deductive explanations, the factual minor premise (e.g., that Smith is both innocent of any offense and in no way a threat to the well-being of others) must benefit from empirical modes of confirmation. There is always room for disagreement over the evidence favoring or challenging the minor premise both in science and in moral discourse.

What clearly distinguishes "moral science" from natural science is neither the form of the explanations nor the criteria applicable to the purely factual part of the respective arguments. The distinction is found in the radically different nature of the major premises themselves. A universal law in natural science predicts future occurrences and can be disconfirmed by them. The law arises from direct observations of natural phenomena and requires exceptionless repeatability of outcomes under relevantly equivalent conditions. But major premises in moral philosophy are prescriptive, not predictive. They declare what ought to be the case, not what is the case. They do not arise from exceptionless and observed natural occurrences and they cannot be confirmed or disconfirmed by any purely empirical phenomenon.

Granting the fundamental differences between moral

premises and scientific laws, we still must take note of the equivalent forms of explanation, for it is this equivalence that removes moral discourse from the realm of mere opinion, private feelings, and popular enthusiasms. The likes and dislikes of persons or groups of persons are of no *moral* consequence whatever unless a major moral premise is stipulated such that a universalized duty or obligation arises from such likes and dislikes. Intuitively we recognize that the rightness or wrongness of murder would not be affected merely on the showing that large numbers of persons "felt" it to be right or wrong. Thus, when we refer to "values" in an attempt to specify whether or not science is value-laden or value-neutral, we must be careful to distinguish between bona fide ethical values—which is to say, *ethics*—and opinions or tastes or social conventions. As I've said, there are ethical presuppositions associated with all scientific activity; presuppositions regarding the requirement of truth; the superiority of rational modes of inquiry over opinion or superstition or conviction; the duty to make knowledge available to others and to publicize it if only so that errors may be detected and removed; the willingness to be constrained by methodological requirements known to promote accuracy and informativeness. One may defend these ethical canons on pragmatic and utilitarian grounds or on deonotological grounds or both, just as one can defend the major premises of moral philosophy on both grounds. But whatever the grounds of defense, the presuppositions themselves are an indisputable feature of the scientific enterprise. Nevertheless, these presuppositions do not in any way determine the actual data resulting from scientific inquiry. Nature is under no compulsion to honor the ethical presuppositions of those who observe and report on natural phenomena. Any "value" the individual scientist has which might lead to distorted observations and reports is a "value" at variance with science's fundamental commitment to *truth*.

There are, indeed, ethical values that surround the labors of science and on which the credibility of these labors depends. In this respect, science is not value-free in its mission or in its internal standards. But it is totally nonevaluative in its proprietorship of the facts of the natural world and in its reportorial and analytical approaches to these facts. This is the nature of science *in principle*. Departures from this constitute malfeasance, and the guilty scientist thus invites rebuke and enduring suspicion.

In light of the essential nature of moral maxims and the difference between these and scientific laws, it should be clear that no fact of science can ever overturn or install the major premises of a moral system. One such fact of science is the measured opinions of persons asked to comment on or judge the desirability of a given course of action. Such opinions, no matter how widely shared, can only be counted as opinions; the percentages stand as no more than a descriptive fact of how responses are distributed in a sample. Even according to the utilitarian calculus, a fact of this kind could not be ethically informing, for the sampled opinions could yield *disutilitarian* consequences if translated into policy. Thus, even on utilitarian construals of ethics, opinion or ephemeral feelings or shifting fashions can never overturn the major utilitarian premises according to which the right course of action is that which is utility-promoting. If this is so of the least traditional of ethical systems, it is doubly so of the more deductive and traditional (Kantian) alternatives.

Some rather odd implications have been drawn from the incommensurability of ethical and scientific laws. There is, for example, the popular view that, because ethical canons cannot be empirically confirmed, they can have no existential standing or they can at most refer to no more than the idiosyncratic sentiments of those who adopt them. Here we have an instance of the externalization of scientific criteria into realms in which these criteria have no place. Note that we cannot confirm *empirically* that true conclusions necessarily follow from true premises in a valid syllogistic argument. This is a logical, not an empirical, truth and thus the empirical criteria of validity are irrelevant. A moral premise of the form, "It is always wrong to X . . ." is a universalized statement which (*therefore*) can never be empirically confirmed. But more to the point, it cannot be empirically disconfirmed either, since it refers to a nonempirical property (the *wrongness*) of a certain class of actions X, To reject the premise is to assert that it is

never necessary to offer *justifications* for doing X and never obliga-
tory to prevent or discourage the performance of X-type actions.
Nor, therefore, would it make any sense to punish those who did
X. But this line of argument culminates in a total skepticism regarding ethical values of any sort, including those that regulate
scientific endeavors. It is an argument that is finally skeptical about
truth itself; about the *duty* to truth. Since such an argument permits or is neutral with respect to fraud and deception, it is an
argument that would rule out even the ethical standards of science.

Setting aside this total skepticism, there is still room
to wonder just what sort of entity an ethical principle is, granting
that it is not "empirical" or, at least, physical. It is a rule-type entity not generically different from entities of the sort, "The Bishop
must be moved only diagonally." Ethical rules regulate social life
and permit, in a manner of speaking, the "game of life" to be played
in harm-limiting, loss-limiting fashion. The game may thus proceed in a way that permits all participants to cultivate their faculties, to add meaning to life, to share in the bounties of society
and civilization. Ethical rules are rules for *humanization*, specifying
tersely those minimal conditions which must obtain if persons are
to realize their potentials and express their best natures. What we
require of the stated maxims of ethics is that they stand in coherent relation to the possibility for a humane and respectful
treatment of others and of ourselves. We require that such maxims, which are constraints on personal autonomy, be *justified* by
being shown to be essential to the larger and more fundamental
objective to which this autonomy attaches itself. Thus, such maxims must be *argued* into being and must make appeals to the rationality—not the senses—of those whose allegiance is sought.
There are to be sure grounds for diagreement over just what the
larger and most fundamental objectives of human autonomy may
be. Thus, there is to this extent a "relativity" in the regulative
maxims of Ethics. But once certain minimum objectives are set—
for example, the immunity of the innocent to punishment, the
freedom to pursue truth and to enter into bonds of friendship and

love with others, protection against unwarranted assaults on our person or unwarranted seizures of our possessions—once these are set, the room for "relativity" is strikingly constricted.

Ethics and Advocacy*

Advocacy in science takes two general forms, one that is explicitly political and another that would present itself as authoritative. In the former case, a professional or scientific association, through its governing boards, speaks out on issues of broad social consequence, hopeful of being heard not because of relevant expertise but only by virtue of the membership's extensive education or presumed intelligence or character. If, for example, the American Meteorological Society were to take a position on, say, affirmative action, the grounds on which the Society might expect recognition would have nothing to do with competence in meteorological research and theory. Such actions, then, are best understood as *pro bono* gestures and are harmful, if at all, only to the extent that they contribute to what is already a rampant sentimentalism in modern approaches to social and political problems.

Advocacy that is advanced on the grounds of authority, however, is quite another matter, for in this case there is the potential for fraud or misfeasance. Psychology is particularly vulnerable here because it is widely recognized as having an authoritative standing where "human" issues are involved. It is not clear to the general public, for example, that the American Psychological Association is no more or less competent to address an issue such as affirmative action than, say, the American Meteorological Society.

There are a few issues on which the APA. has taken

*A version of this section is given in "Ethics and Advocacy," *American Psychologist*, 1984, 39, 787–793.

the advocate's role and which will help to illustrate the schism between fact and value and the dangers of externalizing scientific criteria to nonscientific contexts. The A.P.A. has spoken out corporately on (a) so-called "Gay rights" in the matter of so-called "sexual discrimination"; (b) the Equal Rights Amendment (ERA); (c) alleged "women's rights" in the matter of abortion. I cite these three highly charged areas because they seem to include considerations which psychologists might be generally perceived as having some special competence to address. I will not attempt to reach the right answer on any of these issues. The point in raising them is only to inquire into the ethical dimensions of professional advocacy where issues such as these are involved.

Statutes opposed to hiring homosexuals for certain public employments (e.g., teaching in the lower grades) or to permitting homosexuals certain otherwise private occupations (e.g., the adoption of children) historically arose from a combination of settled principle and arguable fact. The principle was that children, as highly impressionable and malleable persons, must be protected against influences judged to be untoward. The arguable fact is that sexual proclivities are developed in part according to influential adult models and that children regularly exposed to homosexual models may be inclined in the same direction. In a State in which early education is compulsory, the State itself has the special responsibility to ensure that the environments created by it and the institutions it subsidizes and licenses are compatible with the expectations and values of the electorate. These expectations and values must, of course, themselves be compatible with fundamental constitutional principles, but appointment as a teacher or as an adopting parent is not a constitutional right. There are in both instances requirements for eligibility that include "moral character" and fitness to have regular and significant influence on children placed in one's charge.

What has the APA *corporately* to contribute either to the principle or (even) the arguable fact standing behind this issue? Perhaps there are reliable studies to indicate that homosexual teachers and homosexual parents do not have untoward effects on children. Yet, there are also studies strongly suggesting that sexuality is in some measure a *learned* pattern of behavior; that persons are given "sex roles" and come to adopt "sex-role stereotypes" on the basis of social indoctrination. To say the least, then, the factual aspect of traditional policies remains arguable even within the relevant research literature. The only *ethical* stance for a body such as APA would be one that honors the arguable nature of the existing evidence.

But on the separate and very different question of who has *rights* of a given kind, the APA, like the American Meteorological Society, has no special standing at all. Even if the statutes discriminated against persons on racial grounds, the APA, as an association of *psychologists*, would have no relevant expertise by which to take an authoritative position. Opposition to such a policy would have to be grounded not in psychological competence but in moral sensibilities. On the matter of adoption by homosexuals, there might even be circumstances in which the biological parents specify—as a condition of releasing the child to an adoption agency—that the adopting parents be heterosexual or, for that matter, heterosexual Presbyterians. Is it within the professional ambit of psychologists to take an official position on whose rights prevail in such circumstances?

The same presumptuousness is in evidence when APA (along with many other professional groups) declared a boycott on cities whose States had not approved the ERA. As it happens, constitutional scholars quite in sympathy with the objectives behind the Amendment have criticized the specific wording. One can be totally committed to full and equal rights for women without favoring the specific Amendment proposed to achieve it. For an organization such as the APA, therefore, to put its *professional* weight behind this specific Amendment is absurd. Psychological research comparing men and women on any number of performance-tasks has shown and will continue to show that there is no significant difference on some tasks and some significant differences on other tasks where group *averages* provide the basis for comparison. This, of course, has nothing whatever to do with the allocation of *rights* in a just society. We do not reduce the rights of a person on the grounds of that person's being the member of some group which, *on average*, does not come up to the level of some other group *on average*. Such rights or privileges that the law may confer are conferred on *individuals*. From the fact that the majority of men talented enough to play basketball in the National Basketball Association are black, we do not conclude that "Caucasians Need Not Apply."

Ethics proper is simply not carved out of the mountain of often conflicting data amassed by social scientists. The law keeps one eye on ethical principles and the other on relevant facts, but it is aided in neither case by such conflicting data. Psychologists who know this and who still bring corporate and professional pressures to bear on legislation in the domain of rights are committing what can only be called a fraud. And those who do not recognize the difference between the propositional character of ethical-legal argument and the factual character of psychological research are incompetent in a far more damaging respect.

Finally, what might an organization such as the APA be able to contribute to the issue of abortion? There is, alas, a literature in which we will find interesting facts describing the psychological prowess of prenatal and postnatal human beings. There is nothing of a psychological nature that the one-day-old infant can express which is not expressed by the infant two days earlier. To the extent that one's position on the issue turns on whether or not birth *per se* brings about discriminable improvements in mental or behavioral capacities, the psychological findings are germane. But this is not something we need the *corporate* APA to tell us. Nor would the literature itself constitute an argument for or against the alleged right women have to obtain abortions. Mothers do not have the right to terminate the life of children who are psychologically defective. Thus, psychological comparisons of prenatal and neonatal performances are obviously irrelevant to the ethical question of whether life-ending measures are permissible.

So far I have spoken only of corporate advocacy by way of illustrating the externalization of empirical criteria of truth to the domain of nonempirical ethical canons. But psychologists function as advocates one-at-a-time as well, whether as teachers or scientists or practitioners. They are educated men and women who have both the right and the duty to share their knowledge, their wisdom, and even their intuitions with those who may derive benefit from them. But it is precisely because of the authoritative standing they have in one discipline that it is incumbent upon them to make clear whether their writings and utterances are proceeding from that authority. The psychologist who declares that criminals are made and not born receives more respectful attention than a dentist making the same claim. So too with psychologists who speak of the healing powers of positive thinking; of the efficacy of corporal punishment; of the "personalities" of political leaders; of the effects of television on behavior; of the likelihood of a patient, when released, committing a violent crime. The list could be expanded indefinitely. Much of this talk has become loose talk, in part because it is spoken by persons confused as to what they are really *able* to say. Thus:

1. From the fact that empirical studies of "values" turn up significant cross-cultural differences, it does *not* follow that ethical canons are themselves "relative." (Studies showing wide variations across cultures in the sums obtained on arithmetic problems would not sustain the conclusion that the rules of addition are "relative"; only that some people don't know how to add.)

2. From the fact that, *on average*, scores on achievement tests predict later academic success, it does not follow that *this* score will predict the later performance of *this* student.

3. From the fact that h^2 is practically incalculable using human subjects and complex psychological phenotypes, it does not follow that the phenotypes are *not* highly heritable; only that we do not know.

4. From the fact that, on average, children exposed to brutalizing experiences tend to be hostile and aggressive later in life, it does not follow that *this* person's felonious conduct was "caused" by such early experiences.

This list too could be extended indefinitely. Psychological inquiry takes on ethical burdens only to the extent that the discipline's masters speak beyond the perimeter of the known without alerting auditors to the fact. In all significant spheres of human conduct and human thought and feeling, psychological certainties are not to be found. Psychologists speaking on matters psychological are not like physicists speaking on matters physical. We have no unifying and coherent theories vindicated by nearly exceptionless evidence. We have no covering laws worth the name, and only a few empirical laws of any generality. None of this need be a source of embarrassment, and none of it should be camouflaged to create a good impression. Given the state of the discipline, psychologists should be diffident as advocates and grudging in the few generalizations warranted by what we know.

Free Inquiry and the Rights of Others

Owing to the differences between psychological entities and merely physical ones, the former impose constraints on free inquiry that are largely absent in the physical sciences. I refer to psychological entities rather than to persons, because the constraints in question extend to nonhuman species as well. An important question has to do with just how many of the same constraints apply and to what extent. I shall take up this question shortly. But since the entire issue is engaged by the concept of *rights*—whether the "right" to free inquiry or the "right" to be treated in a certain way—it is proper to consider the concept of rights first.

Bentham's famous dictum—that natural rights are but "nonsense on stilts"—impatiently expresses the frustrations endured by those who have attempted to give bulk and meaning to the notion of rights. Any number of standard texts may be consulted for evidence of the continuing ambiguity surrounding the notion,[12] and none of what I had to say in chapter 2 should be taken as conclusive in this vexatious matter. On the construal of legal positivists, a right is no more than the promise made by law to those who, on one basis or another, are regarded as qualified. Thus, such a right is not some abstract feature of the person or some native possession; less is it "natural" in any informed sense of the term. Rather, it is a promised protection extended for purposes of expediency and withdrawn whenever larger social or political considerations demand it. I have elsewhere argued against this view[13] but in the present context it is not necessary to hold to any specific theory of rights. It is enough to recognize that such entities are not "empirical" and can never therefore be sanctioned or illuminated or challenged by science, least of all "social" science. Ethics, as I said earlier in this chapter, arises from certain attributes of human nature, but these are not physical or are at least not reducible to physical attributes. Even on the old Humean theory, according to which the moral categories are grounded in our emotional or sentimental reactions, we are not able to explain either the universalizability of moral canons or our readiness to classify actions as right or wrong independently of our or anyone else's visceral sensations. Nor does the theory explain why the balance of the animal economy—in which there is every evidence of emotional or sentimental impulses—reveals nothing identifiable as a moral prescription.

Without taking sides in the wrangle here, I note only that the rights now claimed by citizens in the Western democracies rest on a sturdy and traditional legal foundation, but one that cannot prevent frequent and even damaging collisions. Society has a right (as it were) to be protected from dangerous persons. Dangerous persons sometimes inform psychologists or psychiatrists or confessors of an intended assault. A "privilege of confidentiality" is alleged by which psychologists, et al. have the "right" not to disclose what a patient or one of the faithful has said. Or, to take another case, persons have a right not to be defrauded. They have, that is, a right to expect that others will not use them for ends of which they are unaware and to which they may very well be opposed. This right presumably covers their privacy such that others have no right to trick them into making known personal matters or personal feelings which they would not voluntarily reveal. But social scientists (and others) have an (alleged) right of free inquiry and this includes research whose objectives might be rendered impossible unless experimental subjects are kept ignorant of or even deceived about the actual aims of the study. Or, finally, persons are thought of as having the right to be spared actions taken against them or constraints imposed upon their autonomy unless they have given an *informed consent* to those interested in or responsible for such actions. But various therapeutic modalities are indefinite in their consequences and thus neither the therapist nor the client can be fully *informed* in a sense that would make *consent* meaningful.[14]

It should be clear that collisions of this sort cannot be fully avoided by means developed within Psychology itself. Because of this, it is somewhat hazardous to rely upon a "professional ethics" as if it were more trustworthy or apt than the more developed and general ethics suffusing long established political and legal institutions. When it comes to settling antagonisms between the aims and practices of a scientific or clinical discipline and this more developed and general ethics, therefore, psychologists should be prepared to confer greater authority on the latter. From an ethical point of view, the fact that an activity occurs within a professional discipline has no bearing on whether it is positive or negative in its ethical "sign." The grounds, if such there be, on which fraud or manipulation or deception or cruelty is wrong are surely wide enough to surround professional actions. If fields such as "biomedical" ethics and "business ethics" are to be apt and useful, their aim should be the weighing of practices in medicine or business against established ethical canons; not the coining of new, untried, and disjointed quasi-principles that happen to make some sort of *ad hoc* contact with medical or business practices. The same is true of "psychological ethics." An action cannot be wrong (morally) in Detroit and right (morally) in Toledo; wrong (morally) in the operating room but right (morally) in the stock exchange. What may differ from setting to setting are conditions that specify the relevant and ruling maxim. The ambiguities surrounding moral assessments have to do with the problem of finding the appropriate principle, not with anything intrinsically ambiguous about the principle itself. I turn now to a specific issue that has animated controversy for decades; an issue that stands as an ethical "hard case" and that illustrates the futility of attempting solutions within the psychological disciplines themselves.

"Animal Rights"

If we remain with the uncontroversial definition of rights as a range of protections conferred by law, we can begin with the *fact of law* that cruelty toward animals is an offense punishable by fine and/or imprisonment depending on the jurisdiction and the severity of the offense. In this purely legal respect, animals have rights; they have the promised protection of law against treatment of a certain kind.

It is not beside the point to inquire if only briefly into the understandings that underlie such legislation. The protection is extended to animals partly on the same grounds as those applying to persons. It is because persons and animals have the *capacity for suffering* that laws are enacted to spare them unnecessary and unjustifiable suffering. Note that the protection is not conditional on the beneficiary's ability to *claim* it. It is claimed in behalf of all potential sufferers by laws that have reached a settled position on the ethical status of cruelty.

We may now ask whether the right of "free inquiry," to the extent that it may collide with protections against cruel treatment, takes precedence over the right to be spared from such treatment. If, for example, free inquiry is on some intelligible and defensible scale of *higher* worth, then the right to engage in studies in which terrible pain and suffering are caused would presumably extend to studies of human beings. Note that the protection itself is grounded in the recipient's *capacity for suffering*. To the extent that this capacity is of comparable magnitude in all of the advanced species, the protection is comparably extended.

Let us say, however, that there is a moral distinction to be made between acts of gratuitous cruelty and those that cause suffering in a way that is unwanted but unavoidable. The sadist tortures a victim for the sadistic pleasures yielded by the act, whereas the scientist is motivated by the quest for truth and would happily abandon pain-producing measures if the quest could be carried through without them. Again, this difference in motives surely would not be sufficient to justify pain-inducing measures brought to bear on human beings. How then might it justify the same measures when confined to creatures that are not human but are still capable of suffering?[15] The answer most frequently given by the scientific community is that human beings are regarded (by human beings!) as having higher moral worth than any and all nonhuman beings. Thus, research capable of reducing *human* suffering is justified even though it must cause suffering to nonhuman organisms.

This, I say, is the common reply, but it is not entirely satisfying. First, it is not clear just how this putative continuum of moral worth is constructed or just how an entity's position on it is determined. There is a definite strain of "species-ism" in the position, not entirely unlike garden varieties of racism and sexism. It surely would not follow, for example, from the fact that we are the most fully evolved or most advanced species that we have a *right* to maim and ravage all other forms of life in our own interest. We are, according to a popular and powerful theory, the most advanced of the *primates*, but we are no more "fully evolved" than dogs are as *canines* or birds as *avians*. Each extant species, including our own, is just where it is on an evolutionary continuum that has not ended.

The only way out of the bind—and it is not a particularly ethical way—is to acknowledge that the entire realm of ethics exists only by dint of human rationality, and that this same rationality has voted for human life and human interests over the life and interests of other species whenever the two are in conflict. Thus, where human life can be enhanced and human suffering diminished by the appropriate use of nonhuman creatures, we vote for ourselves.

To see this as an issue at all, however, is to see the need for a virtually transparent connection between the research and the relief of human suffering or the enhancement of human life. It is not, then, the (alleged) "right" of free inquiry that provides moral justifications for the suffering endured by animal-subjects. Rather, it is a pragmatic standard that is adopted, once we have agreed to give moral precedence to human beings. But this standard is set not by the methods or theories of science; it is set by the expressed needs and desires of the public at large. It is the public that decides, through its legislators, whether the *privilege* to engage in ethically unsettled research is to be granted; whether the promised gains are of sufficient importance in *human* terms to permit actions that would otherwise be unacceptable and unconscionable. They would be unacceptable and unconsciona-ble whenever their only excuse was the private desire of the prac-titioner, even where that desire was aimed at "inquiry" and its resulting satisfactions. It must be granted in this connection that the relationship between much of psychological research and the potential relief of human suffering or enhancement of human life is less than transparent. Some of it is merely habitual and even more of it is prosaic, uninspired, monotonously repetitious, and trivial in its implications. Through it all, tens of thousands of an-imals are crammed into unnatural settings and managed as if they were indistinguishable from inert matter. The temptations to hy-perbole and sentimentalism can be made quite strong by the spectacle of the "vivarium," but they must be resisted. My chief objective here is not to propagandize for a "movement"—there is an Animal Rights Movement—but to clarify the justificatory prin-ciples applicable to research of this type. The principles are not the internal codes of a professional group or caste, but the exter-nal ones that permit society to establish its own priorities, its own best interest. Once this is recognized, psychologists will be less given to huffy and sanctimonious defenses of their craft.

Ethics as a Subject of Inquiry

I referred earlier to the pioneering research of Piaget and the recent work of Lawrence Kohlberg, noting that the num-bers working in this area remain small. I noted, too, that it was only a century ago when the better known writers routinely included the moral dimensions of human life in treatises of a psychological nature. It was a chief objective in chapter 2 to elucidate the incommensurability between scientific laws and explanations of human conduct; in chapter 3, the incommensurability between reductionistic programs and coherent explications of psychological processes. In both instances, the incommensurability becomes especially striking when the psychological side of the equation is occupied by moral terms and actions.

Nonetheless, philosophers indebted to various traditions continue to take firm positions on the nature and even the origin of moral judgments; positions that are either explicitly psychological or at least beholden to one or another folk-theory regarding human psychological attributes. Those writing in that *sentimentalist* tradition made so compelling by Hume are given to believe that the subject-matter of morals is largely exhausted by the feelings or emotions persons customarily experience in response to actions of a certain kind. According to this *emotive* theory, the rational or cognitive side of moral discourse is principally a rationalization of the feelings themselves; an attempt to impose a systematic and logical construction on what, at root, is nothing but felt pleasure or aversion. Philosophers in the rationalist tradition of Kant or the natural-law tradition of Thomas Aquinas[16] insist that the moral domain is irreducibly cognitive and propositional; that it is entered only by creatures able to frame means-ends possibilities; that it is rooted in the ground of intention and purpose. What makes an action good or bad, right or wrong, is thus not a "feeling" created in the actor or in those witnessing or suffering the action but in the *principle* or maxim of which the act is expressive.

Again, Piaget and Kohlberg are among the astonishingly few psychologists to recognize the essential role of psychological inquiry in an issue of this kind. The philosophical disputes are, we must think, accessible to the *facts* unearthed by research into alleged moral "sentiments" and alleged moral "reasoning." It may indeed be the case that the genuinely philosophical aspects of the issue will survive nearly any conceivable finding, but it is only under the light of reliable facts that these aspects can be clearly seen.

It is not my intention here to prejudge the outcome of enlarged research, nor would I suggest that the terms of the philosophical dispute would be significantly altered were psychologists to discover any degree of diversity or uniformity in the manner in which persons come to have various moral inclinations. More than one enthusiast—whether utilitarian or deontologist—has found the *naturalistic fallacy* irresistible and I should not want to lengthen the list on either side. Nonetheless, the discovery that solutions to morally dilemmatic problems display rather abrupt logical discontinuities is suggestive.[17] One would think that a conditioning history linking moral judgments to this or that emotion would produce only variations in what might be called the strength of conviction, not the actual principles on which the conviction rests.

If anything, however, psychologists have mostly ignored the principled basis of evaluative discourse and have focused instead on what must be the least interesting and least informing of facts; *viz*, the statistical incidence of support for various points of view or "feelings." It is not a sign of maturity for a discipline to be preoccupied with "counting heads," as it were, and to avoid the serious question of the variables that come to determine the positions thus polled. What, finally, are the bases upon which persons come to hold moral positions and are they similar to or different from the bases on which beliefs, opinions, and convictions are erected? We can agree in advance that answers to these questions will not simultaneously settle the fundamental question of morals but we can also agree that the psychological and the moral realms are not entirely disparate.

The relative aloofness of psychologists toward moral "phenomena" is but a species of the larger relative indifference to rationality itself. For all the research and theory devoted to "cognitive science," there remains a very wide region of rationality that is neglected. Just a few questions illustrate the point:

1. What are the psychological marks of *knowledge* and how do these differ from the marks of belief or speculation or hunches?

2. Setting aside the Piagetian question of when children comprehend universals, what is the minimum psychological or cognitive equipment necessary for anyone of any age to traffic in universalized propositions?

3. How are abstract concepts represented? In the argot of today's Cognitive Psychology, how are such concepts as imaginary numbers or infinite sets or right and wrong or justice "schematized" or "coded" or "represented"?

Certainly one reason for the short-changing of rationality is that the subject does not lend itself to the normal forms of experimental inquiry, replete with t-tests, computer-generated displays, and the like. Perhaps a more subtle factor is the utter ubiquity of rationality such that, merely to serve as an experimental subject, one is presumed to be in possession of the necessary faculties of reasoning. But this is just as true of research in visual perception or short-term memory, and in neither of these cases has the ubiquity of the requisite faculties prevented sound and informing experimental analyses. But in the matter of rationality—and of one species of it; viz., moral reasoning—attention has been given primarily to developmental and pathological departures from the norm rather than to the norm itself. As of now, we have no systematic study of, for example, individual differences in performance on logical or moral problems. But it is surely plausible to consider such differences to be behind at least some of the well known differences in "personality" or learning or, for that matter, categories of deviancy. (Recall Locke's thesis that *madmen reason rightly from wrong premises.*)

As with the other major topics of this book, the subject of Ethics is included to draw attention to the discipline's penchant for taking for granted what is far from obvious or for neglecting that which may well be central to its larger agenda. I would not, of course, presume to lay out a program of research on moral reasoning, if only because Kohlberg has done as much at least within a limited context. Nor would I seek to legislate a professional ethics for psychologists, though as I have argued above there would seem to be need for greater thought on the part of those who would use the profession for purposes of advocacy. Finally, I certainly do not seek to foist an "animal rights" thesis with missionary zeal or out of a desire to turn off the lights in the laboratory, though, as noted, *our* alleged rights in this area cannot be casually assumed to be boundless or beyond the call for justifications. Psychology turns out to be "value-laden" in more ways than one, even if its attention to values *per se* is sporadic and desultory.

Summary

Discussions within Psychology as to the value-neutral or value-laden nature of scientific inquiry have been deflected by spurious conceptions of "values" and by a somewhat habitual incomprehension of just what it is that makes the physical sciences far less sensitive to such considerations. There has been a general and invalid supposition to the effect that the motives and convictions of scientists are inextricably connected to their actual findings and theories. Thus, a prevailing relativism asserts itself within psychological circles addressing the character and aims of science. This discourse has even moved toward the odd conclusion that a different species of Ethics applies to scientific inquiry; that, since all values are "relative," there are specific values covering the scientific enterprise different from those operating in the nonscientific context.

Unclear as to the nature of Ethics, the psychological establishment has found itself in positions of advocacy where it lacks relevant standing and where it thus invites the charge of fraud or innocence. In the same state of confusion the same establishment has undertaken to articulate justificatory grounds for any number of practices—whether in research or in therapy—but where the grounds themselves are either misplaced or, if thoroughly tilled, portentous. Through it all, Psychology has been surprisingly aloof to those intellectual and rational processes by which persons develop ethical systems. Thus, the attribute that may be our most distinguishing has been neglected by the one discipline whose methods and perspectives would seem uniquely suited to assessments of it.

Notes

1. The Armchair and the Laboratory

1. William James, *Principles of Psychology*, pp. 467–468.

2. Various behavioristic strategies since the time of John Watson have striven without success to achieve a "purely" descriptive system. The adverb here is will-o'-the-wisp. The very commitment to descriptivism is a metaphysical one calling for analysis and justification.

3. Examples are everywhere, but none more to the point than B. F. Skinner's *Beyond Freedom and Dignity*. New York: Knopf, 1971.

4. C. G. Gross, C. Rocha-Miranda and D. Bender. "Visual properties of neurons in inferotemporal cortex of the Macque." *Journal of Neurophysiology* (1972) 35:96–111. It is unlikely that the case is even this simple in the realm of the monkey brain. That a given (single) cell "fires" at a greater rate in the presence of one visual form than in response to others surely does not confer perceptual *experiences* on that cell.

5. A. J. Ayer, *The Problem of Knowledge*, p. 7.

6. In this connection, see my *Systems of Modern Psychology: A Critical Sketch*. In this earlier work I have examined specific and still highly influential approaches to the subject, largely ignoring the *meta-psychological* problems to which the current work is devoted.

7. In borrowing this piece of modern philosophical reasoning I do not mean to stand behind it. The notion of knowledge as "a true belief" or "a belief that the subject is justified in holding" is plagued by difficulties that have not gone unnoticed in the recent philosophical literature. It is useful to note here the difference between the strict philosophical sense of "knowledge" and the looser psychological sense. The psychologist is likely to regard Smith's claimed knowledge as knowledge *simpliciter*, even if Smith happens to be wrong. The psychologist, that is, may have no purpose that requires testing such claims for validity since what is under investigation is the *process* and not the content

per se. Philosophically, of course, it is senseless for Smith to claim "I know about unicorns," since no such entity exists and therefore the knowledge-claim refers to *nothing*. Following Ryle, many have found it useful to distinguish between knowing *how* (e.g., to dance, to drive) and knowing *that* (e.g., the President is elected to no more than two terms). Belief does not enter into the former, which is nonpropositional, but does seem to be inextricably tied to the latter. If Smith *knows* that presidents are limited to two terms, surely he *believes* it. If, however, he believed that three terms were allowed, he could not be said to know it, for it is false. Thus, knowledge and belief are different states of a claimant that are to be evaluated in "justificatory" terms. A little thought is sufficient to show that this will not put the matter to rest!

8. This is found in J. J. C. Smart's "Sensations and Brain Processes."

9. See chapter 11 of Richard Hofstadter's *Gödel, Escher, Bach: An Eternal Golden Braid*. New York: Basic Books, 1979. Throughout this long and oddly composed "fugue," the author is comforted by reducing the dilemma to the discovery of just such "symbols," as if the brain *qua* brain *could* possess them. The search for a neuropsychological Rosetta Stone must be aimless, since brain *qua* brain has no language *qua* language. In the next chapter this issue is examined at some length.

10. This famous analysis is found in ch. 2 of Quine's *From a Logical Point of View*.

11. Robinson, *Systems of Modern Psychology*, ch. 4.

12. I refer, of course, to recent work employing reaction time to assess the time-constants and "processing" nuances associated with cognition. The older "complication experiments" of the Leipzig laboratory were impelled by similar considerations and often involved similar methods.

2. Determinism

1. The works of Aristotle referred to are taken from *The Basic Works of Aristotle*, edited by Richard McKeon. It is in book II, ch. 3 of the *Physics* that the fourfold theory is set forth and used to assess critically older approaches to the problem of causation. Additional discussions and applications appear in *On the Parts of Animals* (639^b–640^a), Book A, ch. 3 and Book Δ, ch. 2 of the *Metaphysics* and (implicitly) in ch. 3 of the *Nichomachean Ethics*, where volition, choice, etc. are examined.

2. In book V, ch. 2 of the *Metaphysics* he leaves no doubt about this: ". . . that for the sake of which other things are tends to be the best and the end of the other things; let us take it as making no difference whether we call it good or apparent good" 1013^b). The same point, in nearly the same words,is made in book II, ch. 3 of the *Physics* (195^a).

3. Book II, ch. 8 of the *Physics* (199^b): "Art does not deliberate. If the ship-building art were in the wood, it would produce the same results *by nature*. If, therefore, purpose is present in art, it is present also in nature."

4. *Nichomachean Ethics*, ch. III.

5. *Politics*, book III, chs. 4 and 5.

6. *Physics*, book II, ch. 8. Action *for an end* is, says Aristotle, present in that which comes to be and is *by nature*, but there are also coincidences. It does not rain *so that* food will rot on the threshing room floor, though the relationship between rain and the *growth* of crops is surely not coincidental.

7. An amplified sense of *natural* necessity requires a separate inquiry into Ar-

istotle's use of the term *nature* (*physics*). See, for example, his discussion in *Metaphysics*, book V, ch. 4.

8. Again, "in the matter" must be understood as not *coincidentally* in the matter or the thing. In book V ch. 6 of the *Metaphysics*, for example, Aristotle notes that the identity implied by "Coriscus is musical" is of an accidental or merely correlational nature. Coriscus is not "musical" in the way that he is a *man*. He is one of the instantiations of the definition of "man" and, to be at all, he would have to be such an instantiation. His being, however, is not conditional upon his musicality.

9. *Physics*, book II, ch. 8 (199^b)

10. In all of Newton's longer treatises, even in Optics, he rarely misses an opportunity to note the divine hand behind the order and lawfulness revealed by his discoveries.

11. I discuss this in *An Intellectual History of Psycholgoy*, rev. ed. ch. 7.

12. John Locke, *An Essay Concerning Human Understanding* (1690).

13. For an excellent and accessible treatment, consult A. A. Luce, *Berkeley's Immaterialism*.

14. George Berkeley, *A Treatise Concerning the Principles of Human Knowledge* (1710).

15. David Hume, *Enquiry Concerning Human Understanding*. 1904.

16. David Hume, *A Treatise of Human Nature*.

17. Hume, *Treatise*, I, III, xv.

18. On Mill's general influence and his debts to Hume, see my *Toward a Science of Human Nature*.

19. There has been a revival of interest in Reid over the past decade or so, and his principal works are now more readily available. See Bibliography. Interpretive essays can be found in vol. 61 (2) of *The Monist* (1978). In the chapter devoted to J. S. Mill in my *Toward A Science of Human Nature*, the Reid-Hume tensions are discussed in relation to Mill's (Humean) war on *intuitionism*, so-called.

20. The most accessible collection of seminal essays on causation is Tom L. Beauchamp, ed., *Philosophical Problems of Causation*. 1974.

21. Immanuel Kant, *Critique of Pure Reason* (A195–196 = B240–241) (1781). For an excellent discussion of the Second Analogy, see L. W. Beck, "Once More Unto the Breach: Kant's Answer to Hume Again."

22. William Kneale, "Universality and necessity."

23. George Molnar, "Kneale's argument revisited."

24. Ibid.

25. Richard Taylor, "Determinism." In *The Encyclopedia of Philosophy*, 2:359.

26. Donald Davidson, "Actions, Reasons and Causes."

27. Davidson's important contributions to this issue are drawn together in his recent *Essays on Actions and Events*. In "Psychology as Philosophy" (pp.229–244) we find Davidson moving away from the somewhat "scientized" arguments of "Actions, Reasons and Causes." For an illuminating discussion of Davidson's earlier and later positions, see John Bishop, "Agent Causation," *Mind* (1983) 92:61–79.

28. The literature on *authenticity* is somewhat scattered and episodic. Recent and informing treatments of the subject are provided by Robert Young, "Autonomy and Socialization" and, in rebuttal, by Marc Bernstein, "Socialization and Autonomy)."

29. On Mill's dilemma in this regard and his reliance on the concept of "character" to solve the dilemma, see my chapter on Mill in *Toward a Science of Human Nature*.

30. Again, his *Beyond Freedom and Dignity* is queer in just this way.

31. In Aristotle the distinction is central to his very concept of "final causes." Leibniz makes the reasons-causes distinction in a number of places and quite explicitly in Sec. XIX of his *Discourse on Metaphysics* where he says this against materialistic attempts to explain significant actions:

> When one seriously holds such opinions which hand everything over to material necessity or to a kind of chance . . . it is difficult to recognize an intelligent author of nature. The effect should correspond to its cause and indeed it is best known through the recognition of its cause, so that it is reasonable to introduce a sovereign intelligence ordering things, and in place of making use of the wisdom of this sovereign being, to employ only the properties of matter to explain phenomena. As if in order to account for the capture of an important place by a prince, the historian should say it was because of the particles of powder in the cannon having been touched by a spark. (G. W. v. Leibniz, *Discourse on Metaphysics*.)

Hegel, of course, raised reason to an active principle of which the very course of human history is expressive.

32. Bernstein, "Socialization and Autonomy."

33. Young, Autonomy and Socialization."

34. Bernstein, "Socialization and Autonomy." p. 123.

35. Davidson, "Psychology as Philosophy"

36. Davidson, *ibid.*, p. 233.

37. *Ibid*

38. This point is paradoxically honored by expressions such as "unconscious motivation." *Motives*, as part of the causal conditions under which agency must operate, need not be *consciously* recognized by the actor or even intelligible to him.

39. Donald Davidson, "How Is Weakness of the Will Possible?" pp. 93–113.

40. *Ibid*, p. 113

3. Reductionism

1. A trenchant expression of this scepticism, still worth reading, can be found in B. F. Skinner's "Are Theories of Learning Necessary?" Although the word "learning" is featured in the title, Skinner's indictment can be directed at all scientific theories of a certain kind. He is especially and effectively critical of theoretical explanations based upon assumed or even observed processes at levels of observation different from the level at which the phenomena to be explained have been observed. Skinner does not, of course, object to statistical inferences from recorded facts or to general mathematical descriptions of them, but such inferences and descriptions are not after all "theories" if all they claim to achieve is a short-hand summary of what has already been observed.

2. The hand-in-glove relationship between sensory physiology and psychophysics is sufficient to defend the general proposition that analytical models are *productive* and not merely descriptive or redescriptive. In the absence of reliable psychophysical data, the experimenter would be hard-pressed to discern which of any of a large number of physiological records constituted the relevant correlate of a given perceptual outcome. Historically, reliable psychophysical findings have directed the course of neurophysiological research in sensory processes. The interdependence is brilliantly set forth in F. Ratliff, *Mach Bands*. Here the Nobel Prize winning efforts of H. K. Hartline on inhibitory mechanisms in the compound eye of *Limulus* are tied together with decades of psychophysical

studies of contrast phenomena. The mathematical model of lateral-inhibitory mechanisms both describes and predicts psychophysical phenomena and does so in the causal manner of genuinely scientific explanations.

3. For A. Turing's own statement of the thesis, see his "Computing Machinery and Intelligence," pp. 433–460. There are at least two Turing-arguments though it is not clear in what sort of relationship, if any, they stand to each other. One has to do with the theoretical proposition that any given decision-process is expressible as a finite number of binary events and is therefore reducible to such events. But "reducible" here is ambiguous. If it is the case that every decision-process is *in fact* composed of such binary events, then the Turing-argument is not reductive but algorithmic. The second argument, to the effect that a true test of "intelligence" or its simulation calls for competent judges to be able to distinguish between the person and the machine is also not a defense of reductionism. If, for example, the person and the machine actually do exactly the same operations in arriving at decisions, then their indiscernibility again cannot be taken as an instance of "reduction."

4. C. H. Graham, "Behavior, Perception and the Psychophysical Methods," pp. 108–120.

5. Ludwig Wittgenstein, *Philosophical Investigations*.

6. The philosophical journals are still alive with interpretive essays on one or another feature of Wittgenstein's teaching. Major exegetical treatments have been provided by J. Griffin, *Wittgenstein's Logical Atomism*; Norman Malcom, *Knowledge and Certainty*; George Pitcher, *The Philosophy of Wittgenstein*. More recently a summoning interpretation has been offered by Saul Kripke in his *Wittgenstein on Rules and Private Language*. My own assessment of the Wittgensteinian dilemma is different from Kripke's in a number of ways and makes much more of the private nature of sensations than Kripke does.

7. Wittgenstein, *Philosophical Investigations*.

8. *Ibid*.

9. *Ibid*.

10. *Ibid*.

11. Note how this concept of *replacement* in Wittgenstein merges with Turing's and, like Turing's, fails to be *reductive*. Assume, for example, that for every early psychological state (S_E) giving rise to an early behavioral expression (B_E), there is ontogenetic replacement by a later behavioral expression (B_L). In what sense can these more recent expressions be regarded as *reductions* of S_E? I submit, *none*. Wittgenstein is working on the wrong side of the functional equation, $B = (f)S$. If there is to be a reduction, the S, not the B has to be pared down, and this cannot be achieved by any program concerned with "replacements" in the B-category.

12. For an instructive discussion of this thesis see Kurt Beier, "Smart on Sensations."

13. Wittgenstein, *Philosophical Investigations*.

14. Very much progress has been made in this area over the past decade, to the point where the deaf now can look forward to devices that deliver coded signals directly to the inner ear. Though now somewhat dated, an instructive introduction to the methods of analysis and to the relationship between sensory research and the technology of communication, see J. C. R. Licklider, "Three Auditory Theories." Along similar lines, consult T. Sterling, E. Bering, S. Pollack and H. Vaughan, eds., *Visual Prosthesis: The Interdisciplinary Dialogue* (New York: Academic Press, 1971).

15. Jerry Fodor, *Psychological Explanation: An Introduction to the Philosophy of Psychology* (especially pp. 124–134).

16. *Ibid.*

17. Wolfgang Köhler, *The Task of Gestalt Psychology.* For a recent philosophical employment of the concept, see ch. 3 of Austen Clark, *Psychological Models and Neurological Mechanism: An Examination of Reductionism in Psychology.* Clark offers three criteria by which psychophysical isomorphism may be regarded as established, none of the three requiring a strict, point-for-point isomorphism or "identity." Generally, isomorphic identities may be assumed when (a) lesion, stimulation and/or pharmacological studies yield causally sufficient relationships between brain processes and psychological processes or functions; (b) when the implicated structures are sufficiently robust to serve as "values of the variable in question"; (c) when on at least some occasions there is direct observation of the psychoneural relationship (p. 96). Even in these modest terms, the thesis of isomorphism seems testable only in limited and *ad hoc* fashion, allowing very little generalization beyond the specific contexts in which the tests proceed.

18. For two wholesomely controversial statements of the position, consult Paul Feyerabend, "Materialism and the Mind/Body Problem" and Richard Rorty, "In Defence of Eliminative Materialism," pp. 112–121. In his "Functionalism, Machines and Incorrigibility," Rorty says that, ". . . if we understand materialism as a possible *replacement* for common sense, then it is obviously true" (p. 219). But his argument really does no more than seek to establish rules for *talking,* which is all that an argument for *replacement* can establish. The mentalist might just as well argue for an *eliminative mentalism* when it comes to hopes, fears, perceptions, thoughts, etc., insisting that, in regard to these states, it is nonsense to refer to neurons, transmitters, etc.

19. A clear modern statement of the thesis is J. J. C. Smart's, "Sensations are Brain Processes."

20. Clark in *Psychological Models* warns against assuming that the failure of a term-for-term reduction implies the failure of an explanation-for-explanation reduction (p. 154). But then he takes "explanation" to involve rendering "some puzzling phenomenon clear or intelligible" (p. 155). What he does not show is that psychological explanations are "puzzling" or that physiological alternatives are somehow more clear or intelligible. As I argue throughout the present chapter, there is a worrisome strain of *unintelligibility* in statements in which neural terms replace psychological ones.

21. R. Puccetti, "The Duplication Argument Defeated," pp. 582–586: "The notion that one could exchange one's *brain* . . . for another and remain the same psychological entity may not be contradictory, but it is scientific nonsense" (p. 582).

22. Both in the final chapter of my *An Intellectual History of Psychology,* and in ch. 4 of J. C. Eccles and D. N. Robinson, *The Wonder of Being Human: Our Brain and Our Mind.*

23. Smart, "Sensations."

24. *Ibid.*

25. For the seminal article, see Saul Kripke, "Naming and Necessity."

26. Eccles and Robinson, *Wonder of Being Human,* ch. 4.

27. J. J. C. Smart, "Sensations."

28. Karl Popper and John C. Eccles, *The Self and Its Brain* (Berlin: Springer-Verlag, 1978); see especially pp. 96–98.

29. Irving Thalberg, "Immateriality," pp. 105–113. The position taken here is one of Wittgensteinian skepticism but I can't see that the author has advanced the philosophical issue very far along.

30. Cf. Kurt Beier, "Smart on Sensations."

31. Central state materialism can be taken as a species of the Identity Thesis

but it could also be phrased in a manner compatible with epiphenomenalism. Perhaps the best general defense of it is Herbert Feigl, The "Mental" and the "Physical": The Essay and a Postscript. It is interesting that philosophical materialists, who often come to modify or even disavow earlier positions, do so in response to no particular scientific finding. It would seem that one's position on this matter is dangerously invulnerable to any fact arising from research on the brain.

    32. Eccles and Robinson, Wonder of Being Human, ch. 4.

4. Explanations

    1. Hempel's influential essays are collected in Carl G. Hempel, Aspects of Scientific Explanation and Other Essays in the Philosophy of Science. Aristotle anticipates the model in several places but most directly in the Posterior Analytics, Book I, Chs. 1–6. For example, in 71^{b}–72^{a} he says, "We suppose ourselves to possess unqualified scientific knowledge of a thing . . . when we think that we know the cause on which the fact depends . . . and . . . that the fact could not be other than it is."

    2. Hempel, "Aspects of Scientific Explanation."

    3. William Dray, who dubbed the nomological-deductive model the "covering law" model, provides an incisive argument against the applicability of such models to historical events. William Dray, Laws and Explanation in History. For a clear statement of the thesis Dray opposes, C. G. Hempel's "The Function of General Laws in History" is still instructive. On conceptual problems with the model, see R. Eberle, et al., "Hempel and Oppenheim on Expanation."

    4. I do not discuss certain lexical dilemmas faced by the model, though some mention here may be useful. A typical objection of this sort is as follows: Suppose we take as a universal law, Water expands when cooled. We now have a sample of water; we observe that it has not undergone expansion and we conclude (deduce) that it was not cooled. Question: Have we explained why? The general problem is one of going from a universal law legislating what is, to an explanation of why it is. Presumably, explanations are replies to interrogatives. From the nonexpansion of water, however, we surely do not know why that water was not cooled, only that it was not. But as I try to show in the chapter, there is a special standing to be assigned to scientific explanations grounded in nomic necessity. Agency plays no part and therefore a nomological explanation is not part of the universe of discourse in which ordinary agency-prone interrogatives occur.

    5. Note that this is not necessarily tied to reasons-causes tensions but is more the sui generis argument for the unique character of personal as well as historical phenomena, or really any phenomena of a nonrecurring and nonreplicable variety.

    6. Enter "final causes". For the immensely influential nineteenth-century argument, consult G. W. F. Hegel, Reason in History: A General Introduction to the Philosophy of History. The influence can be found in R. G. Collingwood's The Idea of History, and surely animates the cited work by William Dray.

    7. Thomas Kuhn's The Structure of Scientific Revolutions has become the more or less official text for this position. For a review of its ambiguities and of Kuhn's own more recent and perhaps shifting allegiance toward it, see his "Reflections on My Critics" in Lakatos and Musgrave, Criticism and the Growth of Knowledge.

    8. Hempel developed this in "The Function of General Laws in History."

9. Karl Popper's position on this is clearly set forth in "Normal Science and Its Dangers."

10. Pierre Duhem's version of the thesis is set forth in *La Theorie Physique, Son Objet et sa Structure* (1905). The English edition is *The Aim and Structure of Physical Theory*. W. v. O. Quine's development of the thesis is given in his *From a Logical Point of View*.

11. I discuss this at some length in the last chapter of *Systems of Modern Psychology: A Critical Sketch*.

12. Clark Hull, *Principles of Behavior*. In the Hullian system, motivation is a drive-reducing operation, but the drives themselves are rooted in tissue-needs and are explicable in exclusively biological terms.

13. David McClelland's *The Achieving Society* is a totally "psychologized" approach to human motivation.

14. Consider only psychoanalytic theories of psychosexual development.

15. A coherent behavioristic account of motivation is provided by B. F. Skinner, *Science and Human Behavior*.

16. Daniel N. Robinson, *Psychology and Law: Can Justice Survive the Social Sciences?*

17. D. J. MacFarland, *Feedback Mechanisms in Animal Behaviour*.

18. Austen Clark, *Psychological Models and Neural Mechanisms: An Examination of Reductionism in Psychology*.

19. The classic study is, of course, F. D. Sheffield and T. B. Roby, "Reward Value of a Non-nutritive Sweet Taste." *Journal of Comparative and Physiological Psychology* (1950) 43:471–481. But even Pavlov's work on fistulated dogs makes the same point.

20. See, for example, McClelland, *The Achieving Society*.

21. For illustrations, see A. Amsel, "Frustrative nonreward in partial reinforcement and discrimination learning"; T. Thompson and W. Bloom, "Aggressive Behavior and Extinction-induced Response-rate Increases," *Psychonomic Science* (1966) 5: 535–536.

22. Psychologists are familiar with the "Butler box" as a device for illustrating the strong curiosity of the monkey. See also D. E. Berlyne, "Novelty and Curiosity as Determinants of Exploratory Behavior."

23. Joseph Rychlak, in *The Psychology of Rigorous Humanism* tries to reconcile teleological and scientific explanations, but with mixed results. Like the psychoanalysts, too many humanistic psychologists deny themselves the full benefits of their approach in order to secure the ever elusive and marginally useful schemes of the developed sciences.

24. Peter Winch, *The Idea of A Social Science*.

25. Collingwood, *The Idea of History*.

26. Hegel, *Reason in History*.

27. Dray, *Laws and Explanation in History*.

28. The entire field owes much to Fritz Heider's *The Psychology of Interpersonal Relationships*. David Schneider now edits the journal devoted to the subject (*Social Cognition*) and numerous books have recently been spawned.

29. Relevant findings are abundant: S. E. Asch, "Opinions and Social Pressure," L. Festinger, "A Theory of Social Comparison Processes," L. Festinger, A *Theory of Cognitive Dissonance*.

30. E. E. Jones, et al. *Attribution: Perceiving the Causes of Behavior*.

5. Ethics and Psychological Inquiry

1. I would refer to volumes in my own edited collection, *Significant Contributions to the History of Psychology* (28 volumes), Washington, D.C.: University Publications of America, 1977–1978. Bain, Wundt, Herbart, Stout, Ward—really all of the nineteenth-century architects of modern Psychology reserved a special place for moral sentiments or moral reasoning or moral impulses. Some (such as Gall and Maudsley and, to a lesser extent, Bain) were inclined to understand this attribute of human mentation as neurologically conditioned whereas others (such as J. S. Mill) chose to address it at the psychological and social levels. But none of the major writers ignored the subject or thought of it as tangential to psychological issues.

2. Jean Piaget, *The Moral Judgment of the Child.*

3. Lawrence Kohlberg, "Development of Children's Orientations Toward a Moral Order."

4. Quantitative measures of this influence are elusive and would probably be misleading. In *Psychology and Law: Can Justice Survive the Social Sciences?* I have shown this influence at work on traditional jural positions regarding the rights of testacy and the presumption of moral responsibility.

5. Thomas Kuhn, *The Structure of Scientific Revolutions.*

6. A recent and coherent statement of this position has been made by P. Manicas and P. Secord, "Implications for Psychology of the New Philosophy of Science," *American Psychologist* (1983)38:399–411. My brief comment on their essay may be consulted: D. N. Robinson, "The New Philosophy of Science: A New Reply to Manicas and Secord." *American Psychologist* (1984)39:920–21. In their essay Manicas and Secord reject both the covering-law model of scientific explanation and what they take to be the Humean theory of causation. Their "new" philosophy of science would replace Hempel's (and Hume's) contingent regularities with a species of *natural necessity* not unlike what I have defended in chs. 2 and 3. But Manicas and Secord misjudge the implications of all this for Psychology and also fail to show how we could ever distinguish between (a) an *unfailing* contingent regularity and (b) natural necessity.

7. See, for example, Leon Kamin, *The Science and Politics of IQ.*

8. An excellent review of the case, though one not entirely distinguished by some of its conclusions, is B. Evans and B. Waites, *IQ and Mental Testing.*

9. The likelihood that $r = +0.771$ will show up when different samples are tested on three separate occasions is too remote for mention. But Gregor Mendel, too, gave us his famous phenotypic ratios—to the nearest whole number—as if these were empirically obtained. His samples were just too small for such exactitude to be forthcoming. Again, Mendel probably saw how the numbers were falling, assembled the theory to account for them and then just applied a "corrective" to the actual data. None of this excuses Cyril Burt, of course, but one wonders whether the many nearly hysterical denunciations directed at him would have been as numerous and as spirited had his statistical arts been in the service of environmentalism.

10. The orderly retreat from relativism has appeared in a number of essays written after the 1962 treatise. See, for example, Thomas Kuhn, "The History of Science."

11. Compare only R. Herrnstein, *IQ in the Meritocracy* with L. Kamin, *Science and Politics of IQ.*

12. Isaiah Berlin, *Four Essays on Liberty*; Felix Oppenheim, *Dimensions of Freedom*; H. L. A. Hart, "Are There Any Natural Rights?"; R. Dworkin, *Taking Rights Seriously*. London: Duckworth, 1977.

13. Robinson, *Psychology and Law*.

14. I have said more on this in both *Psychology and Law*, and in "Therapies: A Clear and Present Danger."

15. It would be convenient to say that suffering that is not intended cannot be the product of *cruelty* since the latter term carries with it the implication of intent. The law itself often ignores this, however, as when a punishment is regarded as "cruel and unusual" quite apart from the intentions of the prison administration or the legislative body. Even in ordinary parlance we are inclined to say that, for example, a child acts "cruelly" when pulling the dog's tail, even if the child does not know the pain thereby caused.

16. These names are illustrative and not intended to suggest historical priority.

17. Kohlberg, "Development of Children's Orientations."

Bibliography

Amsel, A. "Frustrative Nonreward in Partial Reinforcement and Discrimination Learning." *Pyschology Review* (1962) 69:306–328.

Aristotle. *Metaphysics, Nichomachean Ethics, On the Parts of Animals, Physics, Politics, Posterior Analytics.* In *The Basic Works of Aristotle,* Richard McKeon editor. New York: Random House, 1971.

Asch, S. E. "Opinions and Social Pressure." *Scientific American* (1955) 193:31–35.

Ayer, A. J. *The Problem of Knowledge.* Middlesex, England: Penguin Books, 1956.

Beauchamp, Tom L. ed. *Philosophical Problems of Causation.* Encino, California: Dickenson Publishing Company, 1974.

Beck, L. W. "Once More Unto the Breach: Kant's Answer to Hume Again." *Ratio,* 1967 (9):33–37. (Reprinted in Beauchamp, *q.v.*)

Beier, Kurt "Smart on Sensations." In C. V. Borst, ed., *q.v.*

Bender, D., C. G. Gross, C. Rocha-Miranda. "Visual Properties of Neurons in Inferotemporal Cortex of the Macaque." *Journal of Neurophysiology* (1972) 35:96–111.

Berkeley, George. *A Treatise Concerning the Principles of Human Knowledge,* 1710, #90. La Salle, Illinois: Open Court, 1963.

Berlin, Isaiah. *Four Essays on Liberty.* London: Oxford University Press, 1969.

Berlyne, D. E. "Novelty and Curiosity and Determinants of Exploratory Behavior." *British Journal of Psychology* (1950) 41:68–80.

Bernstein, Mark "Socialization and autonomy." *Mind* (1983) 92:120–123.

Bishop, John. "Agent Causation." *Mind* (1980) 89:61–79.

Bloom, W., T. Thompson, "Aggressive Behavior and Extinction-induced Response-rate Increases." *Psychonomic Science* (1966) 5:535–536.

Borst, C. V., ed. *The Mind/Brain Identity Theory*. New York: St. Martin's, 1970.

Clark, Austen. *Psychological Models and Neural Mechanisms: An Examination of Reduction in Psychology*. Oxford: The Clarendon Press, 1980.

Collingwood, R. C. *The Idea of History*. New York: Oxford University Press, 1972.

Davidson, Donald. "Actions, Reasons and Causes." *Journal of Philosophy*, (1963) 60:685–700.

Davidson, Donald. *Essays on Actions and Events*. Oxford: Clarendon Press, 1980.

Davidson, Donald. "How Is Weakness of the Will Possible?" In Joel Feinberg, ed. *Moral Concepts*, Oxford: Oxford University Press, 1969, pp. 93–113.

Dray, William. *Laws and Explanation in History*. Oxford: Orford University Press, 1957.

Duhem, Pierre. *La Theorie Physique, Son Objet et sa Structure*, 1905. The English edition is *The Aim and Structure of Physical Theory*. Princeton: Princeton University Press, 1954.

Dworkin, R. *Taking Rights Seriously*. London: Duckworth, 1977.

Eberle, R., D. Kaplan, R. Montague. "Hempel and Oppenheim on Explanation." *Philosophy of Science* (1961) 28:418–428.

Eccles, John C., Karl Popper. *The Self and Its Brain*. Berlin: Springer-Verlag, 1978.

Eccles, John C., D. N. Robinson. *The Wonder of Being Human: Our Brain and Our Mind*. New York: The Free Press, 1984.

Evans, B., B. Waites, *IQ and Mental Testing*. Atlantic Highlands, New Jersey: Humanities Press, 1981.

Feigl, Herbert. *The "Mental" and the "Physical": The Essay and a Postscript*. Minneapolis: University of Minnesota Press, 1967.

Festinger, L. "A Theory of Social Comparison Processes." *Human Relations* (1954) 7:117–140.

Festinger, L. *A Theory of Cognitive Dissonance*. Evanston, Ill.: Row, Peterson, 1957.

Feyerabend, Paul. "Materialism and the Mind/Body Problem." In C. V. Borst, *q.v.*

Fodor, Jerry. *Psychological Explanation: An Introduction to the Philosophy of Psychology*. New York: Random House, 1968.

Graham, C. H. "Behavior, Perception, and the Psychophysical Methods." *Psychological Review* (1950) 57:108–120.

Griffin, J. *Wittgenstein's Logical Atomism*, Oxford: Clarendon Press, 1964.

Hart, H. L. A. "Are There Any Natural Rights?" *Philosophical Review* (1955): 64:175–191.

Hegel, G. W. F. *Reason in History: A General Introduction to the Philosophy of History*. Translated by R. S. Hartman. Indianapolis: Bobbs Merrill, 1953.

Heider, Fritz. *The Psychology of Interpersonal Relationships*. New York: Wiley, 1958.

Hempel, Carl G. *Aspects of Scientific Explanation and Other Essays in the Philosophy of Science*. New York: The Free Press, 1965.

Hempel, Carl G. "The Function of General Laws in History." *The Journal of Philosophy*, 1942, vol. 39.

Herrnstein, R. *IQ in the Meritocracy*, London: Allen Lane, 1973.

Hofstadter, Richard. *Gödel, Escher, Bach: An Eternatl Golden Braid*. New York: Basic Books, 1979.

Hull, Clark. *Principles of Behavior.* New York: Random House, 1961.

Hume, David. *A Treatise of Human Nature.* London, 1739. L. A. Selby-Bigge ed. Oxford: Clarendon Press, 1973.

Hume, David. *Enquiry Concerning Human Understanding.* London, 1748. La Salle, Illinois: Open Court, 1904.

James, William. *Principles of Psychology,* New York: Henry Holt, 1892.

Jones, E. E., et al. *Attribution: Perceiving the Causes of Behavior.* Morristown, New Jersey: General Learning Press, 1971.

Kamin, Leon. *The Science and Politics of IQ.* Hillsdale, New Jersey: Earlbaum, 1974.

Kant, Immanuel. Critique of Pure Reason (A195–196 = B240–241), translated by Norman Kemp Smith. New York: St. Martin's Press, 1965. Originally published in German in 1781.

Kneale, William. "Universality and Necessity." *The British Journal for the Philosophy of Science* (1961) 46:89–102. (Reprinted in Beauchamp, *q.v.*)

Kohlberg, Lawrence. "Development of Children's Orientations Toward a Moral Order." *Vita Humana* (1963): 6:11–36.

Köhler, Wolfgang. *The Task of Gestalt Psychology.* Princeton: Princeton University Press, 1969.

Kripke, Saul. *Wittgenstein on Rules and Private Language.* Cambridge, Mass.: Harvard University Press, 1982.

Kripke, Saul. "Naming and Necessity." In D. Davidson and S. Harmon eds., *Semantics of Natural Language.* Dordrecht: D. Reidel, 1972.

Kuhn, Thomas. "Reflections on My Critics," pp. 231–278 in, *Criticism and the Growth of Knowledge,* I Lakatos and A. Musgrave eds. Cambridge: Cambridge University Press, 1970.

Kuhn, Thomas. "The History of Science." In D. Sills edition, *International Encyclopedia of the Social Sciences.* New York: Macmillan, 1968.

Kuhn, Thomas. *The Structure of Scientific Revolutions,* Chicago: University of Chicago Press, 1962.

Lakatos, I. and A. Musgrave, eds. *Criticism and the Growth of Knowledge.* Cambridge: Cambridge University Press, 1970.

Leibniz, G. W. v. *Discourse on Metaphysics.* Translated by George Montgomery, with revisions by Albert Chandler. *The Rationalists,* New York: Doubleday, 1960.

Licklider, J. C. R. "Three Additory Theories." In Sigmund Koch, ed. *Psychology: A Study of A Science,* Vol. 1. New York: McGraw-Hill, 1959.

Licklider, J. C. R. *Visual Prosthesis: The Interdisciplinary Dialogue.* T. Sterling, E. Bering, S. Pollack and H. Vaughan, eds. New York: Academic Press, 1971.

Locke, John. *An Essay Concerning Human Understanding* (1690). Chicago: Henry Regnery, 1956.

Luce, A. A. *Berkeley's Immaterialism.* New York: Russell and Russell, 1968.

McClelland, David. *The Achieving Society.* New York: Random House, 1961.

MacFarland, D. J. *Feedback Mechanisms in Animal Behaviour.* London: Academic Press, 1971.

Malcom, Norman. *Knowledge and Certainty,* Englewood Cliffs: Prentice-Hall, 1963.

Manicas, P. and Secord, P. "Implications for Psychology of the New Philosophy of Science." *American Psychologist*, 1983, 38, 399–411.

Molnar, George. "Kneale's Argument Revisited." *The Philosophical Review* (1969) 78:79–89. (Reprinted in Beauchamp, *q.v.*)

Oppenheim, Felix. *Dimensions of Freedom*. New York, St. Martin's Press, 1961.

Piaget, Jean. *The Moral Judgment of the Child*. London: Keagan Paul, 1932.

Pitcher, George. *The Philosophy of Wittgenstein*. Englewood Cliffs: Prentice-Hall, 1964.

Popper, Karl. "Normal Science and Its Dangers." *Proceedings of the Third International Congress for Logic, Methodology, and Philosophy of Science*. Rootselaar and Staal eds. Amsterdam, 1968.

Puccetti, "The Duplication Argument Defeated." *Mind* (1980) 89:582–586.

Quine, W. V. O. *From a Logical Point of View*, Cmabridge: Harvard University Press, 1953; rev. ed., 1961.

Ratliff, F. *Mach Bands*. San Francisco, Holden Day, 1965.

Reid. *An Inquiry into the Human Mind on the Principles of Common Sense* (1764). Timothy Duggan ed. Chicago: University of Chicago Press, 1970.

Reid. *Essays on the Active Powers of the Human Mind* (1788) and *Essays on the Intellectual Powers of Man* (1785). Baruch Brody ed. Cambridge: MIT Press, 1969.

Roby, T. B., F. D. Scheffield. "Reward Value of a Non-nutritive Sweet Taste." *Journal of Comparative and Physiological Psychology* (1950) 43:471–481.

Robinson, D. N. *An Intellectual History of Psychology*. New York: Macmillan, rev. ed., 1981.

Robinson, D. N. *Psychology and Law: Can Justice Survive the Social Sciences?* New York: Oxford University Press, 1980.

Robinson, D. N. *Significant Contributions to the History of Psychology*, (28 volumes), Washington, D. C.: University Publications of America, 1977–1978.

Robinson, D. N. *Systems of Modern Psychology: A Critical Sketch*. New York: Columbia University Press, 1979.

Robinson, D. N. "Therapies: A Clear and Present Danger." *American Psychologist* (1973): 28:129–133.

Robinson, D. N. *Toward a Science of Human Nature*. New York: Columbia University Press, 1982.

Robinson, D. N. "The New Philosophy of Science: A Reply to Manicas and Secord." *American Psychologist*, 1984, 39, 920–921.

Robinson, D. N. "Ethics and Advocacy." *American Psychologist*, 1984, 39, 787–793.

Rorty, Richard. "Functionalism, Machines and Incorrigibility." *Journal of Philosophy* (1972) 69:203–220.

Rorty, Richard. "In Defence of Eliminative Materialism." *Review of Metaphysics* (1970) 24:112–121.

Rychlak, Joseph. *The Psychology of Rigorous Humanism*. New York: John Wiley, 1977.

Skinner, B. F. "Are Theories of Learning Necessary?" *Psychological Review* (1950) 57:193–216.

Skinner, B. F. *Beyond Freedom and Dignity*. New York: Knopf, 1971.

Skinner, B. F. *Science and Human Behavior*. New York: Macmillan, 1956.

Smart, J. J. C. "Sensations are Brain Processes." In The Mind/Body Identity C. V. Borst ed., q.v.

Taylor, Richard. "Determinism." The Encyclopedia of Philosophy, Paul Edwards, editor in chief, 2:359.

Thalberg, Irving. "Immateriality." Mind (1983) 92:105–113.

Turing, A. "Computing Machinery and Intelligence." Mind (1950) 69:433–460.

Winch, Peter. The Idea of A Social Science. London: Routledge Kegan Paul, 1958.

Wittgenstein, Ludwig. Philosophical Investigations, Oxford: Blackwell, 1953.

Young, Robert. "Autonomy and socialization." Mind (1980) 89:565–576.

Index

Critical Assessments of Contemporary Psychology
Daniel N. Robinson, Editor